CORONATION STREET
CELEBRATING 30 YEARS

CORONATION STREET
CELEBRATING 30 YEARS

GRAEME KAY

WITH ADDITIONAL MATERIAL BY
ANTHONY DAVIS AND ANTHONY HAYWARD

Boxtree

Published in association with Granada Television

ACKNOWLEDGEMENTS

The publishers would like to thank the following
for their help in the making of this book:

David Liddiment, Mervyn Watson, Daran Little, Sue Scott,
Delanie Kay, Kathryn de Bell, Anthony Hayward,
Anthony Davis and the cast of Coronation Street.

This book is dedicated to the memory of Graeme Kay.

First published in 1990 by Boxtree Limited

© Boxtree Limited 1990
Photographs © Granada Television

Designed by Roger Kohn
Jacket design by Paterson-Jones
Jacket photographs by Steven Morris
Picture research by Delanie Kay, Kathryn de Bell and Daran Little
Typeset by Rowland Phototypesetting Limited
Bury St Edmunds, Suffolk
Printed and bound in Italy through OFSA for
BOXTREE LIMITED
36 Tavistock Street
London WC2E 7PB

British Library Cataloguing in Publication Data

Kay, Graeme, *d.*1989
Coronation Street, 30 years.
1. Television drama series in English
I. Title   II. Davis, Tony   III. Hayward, Anthony
IV. Granada Television
791.457

ISBN 1-85283-292-4

CONTENTS

INTRODUCTION

For thirty years, *Coronation Street* has been Britain's top TV programme. It is loved by millions and praised by critics for the quality of its writing and acting. Melvyn Bragg called it 'the most professional product of television this country has ever known'. The late Poet Laureate, Sir John Betjeman, said, 'Manchester produces what to me is *The Pickwick Papers*. That is to say, *Coronation Street*. Mondays and Wednesdays, I live for them. Thank God, half past seven tonight and I shall be in paradise.' The late Lord Olivier was another loyal fan. What prompted this attention and praise was a television serial launched at 7pm on Friday, 9 December 1960, with no advance ballyhoo and scheduled to run for twelve episodes. Its success made it a long-running hit not only in Britain, but around the world.

William Roache was in the first, live episode, playing Ken Barlow then, as now. Ken was seen at No 3 with his parents, Frank and Ida, wearing a new navy blue pullover his mother had knitted him, and being hauled over the coals by his tightfisted father for 'throwing away money' by arranging to meet new girlfriend Susan Cuningham in the posh Imperial Hotel. William confesses to having been absolutely terrified that night. 'We all were,' he says. 'When a scene is going out while you are actually doing it, you can't make a mistake. Not one of us knew how the programme would turn out. But here we are, still going strong.'

Anne Kirkbride, who plays Ken Barlow's estranged third wife Deirdre, was a viewer. 'I was just a little girl, six years old, and I remember my mother telling me that there was a new programme starting that night on television and, if I was a good girl, I could stop up and watch it. I can still see myself now, sitting on the edge of the sofa, watching that first episode.'

Elizabeth Dawn, the *Street*'s Vera Duckworth, watched the first programme at her parents' home. 'I thought it was great because it got right down to the nitty-gritty of life,' she says. 'You could identify with the characters because they weren't ladies wearing fox furs; they were very real, ordinary people – and that Ena Sharples was a revelation. At the time, I had a job in a clothing factory and had no thoughts of being an actress, so it never crossed my mind that one day I would actually be in the *Street* myself.'

William Tarmey, Elizabeth's screen husband, Jack Duckworth, was working as an asphalter in the building trade. 'I was 20 and newly engaged, and I spent Friday nights with my wife-to-be at our local cinema, the Poplar, in Failsworth,' he recalls. 'All our courting nights were spent at the pictures, so I didn't see the start of the *Street*.'

Johnny Briggs, who plays Mike Baldwin, was actually in the Granada TV studios in Manchester, where the *Street* is made, but in a different studio, appearing with Judy Cornwell and John Thaw in a drama series, *The Younger Generation*. 'So, although I was on the premises, I never got to see the early episodes,' he says.

Coronation Street has created viewing records. It has been heaped with awards. It has inspired other serials – including *Peyton Place*, which was America's first peak-time serial. It has been studied by academics. Three *Coronation Street* artists – alas, one now dead – have been honoured by the Queen, Violet Carson being made an OBE, and Doris Speed and Jack Howarth MBEs. In 1982, the Queen visited *Coronation Street* with Prince Philip, walking along the newly built outdoor location set and meeting members of the cast grouped at the front doors.

Over the years, the *Street* has also been seen in Holland (where some children learned to speak English with a Lancashire accent as a result of *Street* addiction), Hong Kong (where it was subtitled, with Chinese characters displayed vertically down the left-hand edge of the screen), Nigeria, Singapore, Gibraltar, Greece, Sweden, Belgium, Finland, Denmark, Sierra Leone and Thailand. It has always been among Granada's top ten selling programmes.

In 1989, it gained an omnibus edition and a third weekly episode. And now it is thirty. Not out.

▲ *The Queen, one of* Coronation Street*'s biggest
fans, tours the newly built outdoor set in 1982. Its
authentic look was achieved with 49,000 old
bricks from Salford streets and 6,500 reclaimed
roofing slates*

IN THE BEGINNING –
TONY WARREN

After the first episode of *Coronation Street* was broadcast, one TV critic wrote: 'The programme is doomed from the outset – with its signature tune and grim scene of a row of terraced houses and smoking chimneys.' But that critic had reckoned without the perception of a vividly articulate Northern writer whose fine ear for everyday dialogue and brilliant observation instantly made the programme a winner with the public. Tony Warren, who wrote the first 12 episodes, was the *Street*'s creator. Born in Eccles, a suburb of Manchester, he had grown up with a love of theatre and made his acting debut on radio at the age of twelve in *Children's Hour*. It was there that he met Violet Carson, the programme's 'Auntie Vi', who was to become the hairnetted dragon Ena Sharples in *Coronation Street* many years later. He tried to pursue a stage career in rep but he was growing away from acting and unemployment encouraged him to try his hand at writing.

One day in 1958, Tony visited casting director Margaret Morris at Granada Television, the ITV company for the North West. She dismissed him as an actor but warmed to his inclination towards writing, and arranged a meeting with Harry Elton, one of a group of Canadian TV producers imported by Granada to find talent. 'Without Harry, *Coronation Street* would never have got off the ground,' acknowledges Tony. The budding young writer was commissioned to write some episodes of the ITV detective serial *Shadow Squad*. Six months later, Harry Elton found him a staff job in the promotions department, writing scripts for the announcers. Then, he was given a one-year contract as a writer. His first job was to adapt the Captain W. E. Johns *Biggles* stories for TV, but he pleaded to write about what he knew – the theatre and the North of England. Looking out of his office window across Salford, with its grimy mills and rows of back-to-back terraced houses with smoking chimneys, Harry Elton said, 'What about the story of a street out there?'

Tony, of course, had already had the same idea and submitted it to the BBC, with the title *Our Street*. He received only an acknowledgement slip. Now, with the working title *Florizel Street*, Tony wrote a new script overnight. It was the late Fifties, and books, theatre and cinema had begun to reflect working-class culture in a way that had not been seen before. Tony Warren was to do the same for television. He did not come from a Coronation Street himself, but his grandmother did and, as a child, he visited her and observed the residents. 'Even as a small boy, I used to invent family dramas in my mind and write stories around them,' he says. He eavesdropped on conversations on buses and in pubs, cafés and snack bars. In a memorandum to Harry Elton, Tony described his programme as: 'A fascinating freemasonry, a volume of unwritten rules. These are the driving forces behind life in a working-class street in the north of England.

The purpose of *Florizel Street* is to examine a community of this nature, and to entertain.'

Granada commissioned Tony to write twelve episodes, with a possible bulldozing of the street planned for a thirteenth. When it became clear that the serial would run and run, the programme's first producer, Stuart Latham – known as Harry – proclaimed that Tony's scripts were of a quality and originality he had never previously encountered. Sadly, ten years on, Tony found himself unable to conform to the rigid disciplines and demands of his 'monster' TV success, so he and Granada parted company. He now concludes that he was faced with too much success too soon. 'No 23-year-old could handle the sort of fame that followed,' he says. But he was reunited with Granada and today, back in the bosom of the *Street*'s family of actors and production staff, Tony's credit appears on screen again, although he no longer writes for the programme. He can look back on a flash of genius and inspiration that created television's top programme.

▼ *Tony Warren takes pride in his creation*

▲ *Minnie Caldwell's birthday party in the Rovers, September 1966.*

THE BIRTH OF A LEGEND

Before Tony Warren's baby made its bow in public, there were buckets of blood, sweat and tears to be shed by the tiny production team fighting to give it life. Harry Latham, the producer, was just a freelance director on a one-year contract to Granada TV, but he dedicated himself completely to Tony's idea and highly colourful scripts. The project almost foundered at the first hurdle. What could Granada's casting department, based in London, know about down-to-earth Northern life and the validity of a Salford accent? Fortunately, Harry Latham secured the services of casting director Margaret Morris and her assistant, Jose Scott, who had been an actress in Northern repertory theatre.

To most actors, it was just another twelve-week job before moving on to something else. Tony knew several of the actresses he wanted in the programme, hav-

ing worked with Doris Speed and Violet Carson, and admired Pat Phoenix. Doris was to play Rovers Return landlady Annie Walker and Pat auditioned for the role of buxom Elsie Tanner. 'I was very arrogant at the audition because I didn't think I had a chance of landing the role,' Pat recalled years later. 'When the producer asked me to take my coat off, I said: "You'll just have to bloody well guess, won't you?"' Pat, who was to become one of the *Street*'s legendary characters, was renowned for her fiery temperament and used to producers telling her she was 'too big, too busty and too passion-

ate' for most British TV roles. Fortunately for her, that description exactly fitted Tony Warren's vision of Elsie Tanner, and the role was hers.

The part of Elsie's son, Dennis, was one of those where the production team had difficulty choosing between two or three ideal candidates. Philip Lowrie landed the role after a camera-test separated him from Kenneth Farrington, who became Annie and Jack Walker's son Billy. When Frank Pemberton heard that Granada was prepared to pay £40 a week for 'a middle-aged dad with a genuine Lancashire accent', he raced down to the TV centre and was offered the role of Frank Barlow, Ken's father, on what he later described as 'the most exciting day of my life'.

Others arrived in a more relaxed frame of mind. Jack Howarth, already a 64-year-old showbusiness veteran, had just ended a lucrative 14-year run as Mr Maggs in BBC radio's *Mrs Dale's Diary*. Jack took the part of Albert Tatlock, the cantankerous, be-medalled First World War old sweat in his stride.

Slowly, the jigsaw was coming together, but one key piece was missing. Who could possibly play the scowling old battleaxe, Ena Sharples. A parade of 'thin-lipped little shrews' was scrutinised and thought to be wrong, with time running out. Suddenly, Tony remembered the fearsome actress who had crossed his path as a precocious child actor in *Children's Hour*. But, typically, Violet was not particularly impressed with

▲ *Frank Barlow and aspiring son Ken's battles took place over the HP sauce*

◀ *As* Coronation Street *gained viewers worldwide, Violet Carson flew to meet fans in Nebraska*

▼ *H. V. 'Harry' Kershaw began on the programme as a writer and later became producer*

the character of Ena. 'She amounts to nothing more than a back-street bitch,' she told Tony. When it was suggested that the role might be too difficult for her to play, she changed her tune. 'Don't be ridiculous,' said Violet, who was born in German Street, Manchester, a real Coronation Street, 'I have lived with this woman all my life. There is one in every street in the north of England.' A show was born. In all, 500 hopefuls had auditioned, but only 24 made it.

As Episode One approached, the production team had been strengthened with the arrival of H. V. 'Harry' Kershaw, who was to become a key member of the scriptwriting team and, later, producer. But one problem remained – what about the programme's title? As late as November 1960, just a month before it was due to start, the serial was still known as *Florizel Street*. In Tony Warren's bedroom hung a picture of Prince Charming hacking his way through the enchanted forest to his sleeping princess. And the princess's name? Florizel. But, when one cast member pronounced it 'Flor-izal', the resemblance with a disinfectant was too close to ignore and a fierce debate began over the shortlist of alternatives, *Jubilee Street* and *Coronation Street*. The three Harrys – Latham, Elton and Kershaw –

burned the midnight oil and, when dawn broke, Elton and Kershaw went to bed triumphant, having voted for *Jubilee Street*. Imagine their surprise when a memo from Harry Latham subsequently proclaimed that the new serial would be known as *Coronation Street*.

The next task was to give the programme a home. Designer Dennis Parkin set off with Tony Warren on a tour to find a real-life prototype. In the Ordsall district of Salford, they discovered Archie Street, a row of seven turn-of-the-century, back-to-back dwellings with a pub at one end and a corner shop at the other. In the studio, Dennis's meticulously detailed version of Archie Street was reproduced down to the cobblestones painted on the floor. Alas, the real Archie Street was later bulldozed in the name of progress to make way for high-rise flats.

The script was written, the cast and studio were ready. All that remained was for that first episode to be broadcast live – as all television was in those days – to a waiting nation. No one had predicted the sensational impact it was to have on viewers. Tony Warren and all those who gave birth to *Coronation Street* waited in nervous anticipation . . .

THE SIXTIES

▲ *Emily Nugent, watched by Lucille Hewitt and Dennis Tanner, manages Gamma Garments, a Weatherfield shop*

At 7pm on Friday, 9 December 1960, Eric Spear's air on a trumpet signalled the beginning of a new television serial. Tony Warren's colourful characters were transformed into reality, and the impression they created is as stunning to see today as during that first screening thirty years ago. The programme started with a scene of two children playing in the street outside the corner shop, out of which Elsie Lappin walked to look up at the sign with her name on it. She went back in and said to Florrie Lindley, who had just bought the shop from her, 'Now, the next thing you want to do is get a signwriter in. That thing above the door'll 'ave to be changed.' Elsie Tanner was introduced having a row with son Dennis and later she was seen looking in the mirror and saying to herself, 'Eh, you're about ready for the knacker's yard, Elsie.' Ken Barlow was a young student and arguing with the working-class father from whom he was trying to grow away. Later, Albert Tatlock, the uncle of Ken's future wife Valerie, told him, 'I never thought the day'd come when I'd 'ave to say this, but that college 'as turned you into a proper stuck-up little snob, Kenneth Barlow.' Rovers Return landlady Annie Walker stamped her authority by refusing Dennis Tanner credit on a packet of cigarettes, and Ena Sharples's entrance was nothing short of dramatic. 'I'm Mrs Sharples,' she said, introducing herself to Florrie Lindley in the corner shop. 'I'm a neighbour. Are you a widder woman?'

The characters were sharply drawn and the potential for a long-running saga was clear, but newspaper reviews were mixed after that first episode. The *Daily Mirror* forecast doom and an early departure, but *The Guardian* proclaimed that the programme would run for ever. The public reaction ensured that *Coronation Street* would remain a twice-weekly event, and there would be no bulldozing thirteenth episode. Although not all ITV regions broadcast the *Street* initially, all parts of Britain were following the new serial by the following spring.

It was Ena Sharples who perpetrated the first scandal in *Coronation Street*, one month after its start, although her misdemeanour wouldn't raise an eyebrow these days. Her offence, as caretaker of the Glad Tidings Mission Hall, was to be seen by teetotaller Leonard Swindley drinking in the Rovers Return Snug. Ena offered the classic 'medicinal purposes' defence, but the anxiety brought on a stroke and, consequently, she was involved in the *Street*'s first cliff-hanger. She collapsed in the vestry and was taken to Weatherfield Hospital.

Weddings make wonderful programme fodder and 1961 produced two. The historic 'first' featured Joan Walker, daughter of haughty Rovers Return landlady Annie, who married teacher Gordon Davies and looked splendid on the arm of adoring dad Jack. The lace handkerchiefs were out again in October 1961, after Irish barmaid Concepta Riley said 'I do' to bus inspector and shy widower Harry Hewitt on a coach trip to the Blackpool illuminations. What viewers didn't know at the time was that the two actors involved, Ivan Beavis and Doreen Keogh, were themselves destined to fall in love and marry.

The *Street* suffered a crisis when, in November 1961, Equity, the actors' union, went on strike in a protracted pay dispute with ITV and a ban temporarily eliminated all cast members, apart from the baker's dozen or so who were on long-term contracts. Early *Street* scriptwriter John Finch remembers the dilemma well. 'At one point, we had no actors to serve drinks in the Rovers,' he says. 'One of the stage hands, unseen, used to send pints of beer sliding along the bar-top into vision. It was hilarious, but nerve-wracking at the time because we had no idea how long the dispute was going to last. Harry Hewitt was often seen shouting upstairs to an invisible Lucille, and Annie Walker was pictured constantly in tight close-up because there was no one behind her chucking darts in the vault.'

Producer Derek Granger – later to make *Brideshead Revisited* for Granada TV – came up with a truly original solution. He commissioned a storyline in which Dennis Tanner arrived home with a chimpanzee. Then a snake turned up, and so Granger was slowly supplementing the missing human element in the programme with visiting 'artists' from Belle Vue Zoo. If the union had no answer to that, it quickly pounced when the enterprising Granger started using non-Equity youngsters as under-age milkmen and the like. But it's an ill wind. The strike was biting so deeply in other areas of TV drama that the viewing figures for Granada's twice-weekly serial accelerated further.

More than any other programme, *Coronation Street* has consistently proved that a soap opera is bigger than any actor in it and can survive the departure of even its apparently leading characters. During the so-called bloody purge of 1964, several stalwarts of the programme disappeared for good, one of them in controversial circumstances. Legend has it that new young producer Tim Aspinall, anxious to inject fresh blood into the serial, ordered the death of harridan Martha Longhurst, the old shrew who gathered in the Snug of the Rovers Return with Minnie Caldwell and Ena Sharples rather like the three witches in *Macbeth*. Protests from the cast themselves, largely from Violet Carson and Peter Adamson, were apparently ignored. Right to the end of rehearsals, Adamson refused to say the line 'She's dead', believing in divine intervention, or at least a phone call from Granada TV boss Cecil Bernstein, protector and benefactor of the *Street*. No call came. Thus Martha slumped to her death from a heart attack, over a bottle of Newton and Ridley's milk stout. Martha's death, and actress Lynne Carol's departure, was later recognised as the biggest mistake ever made in the history of the programme. Cecil Bernstein told Violet Carson some years later that it was a regrettable move. She snapped: 'Well, it's too late now, isn't it?'

Noel Dyson, originally cast as Ken Barlow's mother, felt quite differently about her dramatic exit. When the scriptwriters arranged for her to perish under the wheels of a bus, Noel was perfectly happy with the plan. She thought that opportunities for her particular character were too limited. Frank Pemberton carried on for a while as widower Frank Barlow, but both character and actor disappeared when the script conference produced a premium-bond winning storyline that saw Ken's father retire to Wilmslow, Cheshire.

Other casualties of the period included Harry and Concepta Hewitt, and Leonard Swindley, the fussy little draper who was transferred to the head office of Gamma Garments. Few actors have left *Coronation Street* and made the leap to stardom elsewhere, but Arthur Lowe was one of them. Oddly, Captain Mainwaring, the puffed-up little bank manager he played in *Dad's Army*, was not unlike pompous, old windbag Swindley. Arthur was a shy, retiring actor in his *Coronation Street* days and detested publicity. He was in his mid-fifties when he joined the *Street* and turned sixty at the pinnacle of his success in khaki. He was a kindly man whose superb timing and deadpan comedy technique made him one of the great cornerstones of those early, vintage *Street* episodes.

As some stars left, however, others were just emerging. The Ogdens – Hilda, Stan and Irma – put a £200 deposit on No 13 Coronation Street in June 1964. As the workshy Stan, Bernard Youens created a boozy, potbellied layabout who became uncrowned

▶ *Leonard Swindley accuses Ena Sharples, caretaker of the Glad Tidings Mission, of intemperance for drinking a stout in the Rovers and she resigns*

king of the non-working classes, a shiftless yob as Northern as black pudding. Ironically, Bernard wasn't even a Northerner – he came from Brighton, in Sussex. He had a solid background in repertory theatre and had joined Granada Television originally as a velvet-voiced studio announcer. His young partner over the airwaves at the time was the late BBC radio broadcaster Ray Moore. Bernard slipped into another studio for an audition on the off-chance that there might be a job, and the rest is history. Over twenty years, he turned fat Stan into the loafer the nation loved. 'He is my creation – and I am proud of him,' he said. At the height of his fame, Bernard had his own fan club, which voted him 'The Greatest Living Englishman'. Great 'Oggie' storylines of the Sixties included the October 1964 episodes when Stan took up wrestling and was counted out after being thrown from the ring, Christmas Day on the dole in 1966, when he was made redundant from his milk round, and September 1969, when he became a 'primitive' sculptor.

There were many other characters who came and went in the Sixties. Elsie Tanner's daughter Linda and her Czech husband Ivan Cheveski – played by Anne Cunningham and Ernst Walder – had an on-off marriage, punctuated with stormy rows and reconciliations. Linda mysteriously fell downstairs while pregnant, but her son Paul was safely born in June 1961. The Cheveskis emigrated to Canada when Paul was six months old, but

Ivan returned home to Birmingham when Linda left him for another man. In 1984, she returned to *Coronation Street* briefly before resuming her relationship with Ivan.

Lucille Hewitt – actress Jennifer Moss – was the *Street*'s first teenage rebel. Her schoolteachers were outraged when she turned up for lessons with an urchin blonde hairdo and a tattoo on her arm. Born in 1949, she was the rebellious daughter of bus driver Harry Hewitt, a widower who hadn't a clue how to deal with a rebellious young female. He was too wrapped up in his new life with second wife Concepta Riley, whom he married in 1961. And it was Jack and Annie Walker who took little Lucille under their wing, treating her like a second daughter.

▲ *Lucille Hewitt lodges at the Rovers after her father and stepmother move to Ireland*

◄ *After a gas leak, residents are moved to the mission hall for the night*

▼ *Ken Barlow marries Valerie Tatlock, niece of grumpy Albert, and they honeymoon in London*

▲ *There's a grand day out for residents when Emily Nugent organizes a trip to Tatton Park*

▶ *Elsie Tanner weds US Army Master Sergeant Steve Tanner, but tragedy is not far away*

The impetuous Lucille eloped with Gordon Clegg, but he called off their wedding, became a vegetarian and joined a hippy commune somewhere in London. Later, older and wiser, she moved to Ireland to join Harry Hewitt's widow Concepta in Castle Blaney.

One of the first disturbing storylines to rear up in those early days involved Christine Hardman – played by Christine Hargreaves – who suffered a nervous breakdown and had to be talked down from the factory roof by Ken Barlow during an attempted suicide bid. Bad luck dogged Christine – she married Colin Appleby, who was later killed in a car crash. Still looking for

an anchor in life, she became engaged to Ken Barlow's widower father Frank, but it was clear that the age difference would never work and, when they called off the wedding in 1963, she left the *Street*.

Romance was never far away from Elsie Tanner. She was already estranged from first husband Arnold and awaiting divorce when the programme began. Soon, she fell for Chief Petty Officer Bill Gregory – actor Jack Watson – but found out he was married, something he never quite had the courage to tell Elsie. In 1967, Elsie married US Army Master Sergeant Steve Tanner, but they had already split up when he was murdered by another soldier the following year.

▲ *Hilda Ogden finds daughter Irma and son-in-law David Barlow considering a move to Australia and away from the corner shop they own*

◀ *Away from the Rovers Snug, the gossiping street triumvirate of Minnie Caldwell, Ena Sharples and Martha Longhurst still have plenty to talk about*

Ken Barlow's brother David – played by Alan Rothwell – married Stan and Hilda Ogden's scatterbrained daughter Irma. They ran the corner shop together until they emigrated to Australia in 1968. Leslie and Maggie Clegg – John Sharp and Irene Sutcliffe – took over the shop, but his alcoholism made their marriage stormy. Only later did viewers find out that son Gordon – played by Bill Kenwright – was, in fact, the illegitimate child of Rovers Return barmaid Betty Turpin (Betty Driver), whose sister Maggie had brought him up to give him a good name.

The Rovers Return Snug was occupied in the early days by a triumvirate of Ena Sharples, Martha Longhurst and Minnie Caldwell. Even after Martha's death, it remained the place for Ena and Minnie to exchange gossip. Minnie, played by Margot Bryant, also found comfort in her cat Bobby and, for a while, lodger Jed Stone (actor Kenneth Cope), an ex-convict who called her 'Ma'. Although she knew he had served time, she would not hear a word against him. The law finally caught up with him for receiving stolen blankets, and Minnie was heartbroken when he was sent to jail.

Characters such as Ena Sharples, Minnie Caldwell, Elsie Tanner, Annie Walker and Albert Tatlock created a slice of unforgettable television in the Sixties – and, of course, they were seen in glorious black-and-white.

THE SEVENTIES

▲ *The prize of a package holiday to Majorca in a spot-the-ball contest brings sun into the life of Betty Turpin, Emily Bishop, Hilda Ogden, Rita Littlewood and Mavis Riley*

As *Coronation Street* entered the Seventies, it was essential viewing not only in Britain, but around the world. People in Thailand, Sri Lanka, Singapore and Sierra Leone cottoned on to the quaint pearls of Albert Tatlock and company courtesy of subtitles. The natives of the Polynesian island of Oahu, where the TV series *Hawaii Five-O* was made, preferred watching the matrimonial antics and bickerings of Jack and Annie Walker. In 1971, a Canadian television station bought 1,142 episodes of the *Street*, a feat that made the *Guinness Book of Records*.

Deaths and marriages dominated many of the Seventies storylines. David and Irma Barlow had already emigrated to Australia, but tragedy struck when David and son Darren were killed in a car crash. Actor Alan Rothwell, who played David, was to become a familiar face as drug-addict Nicholas Black in another serial, *Brookside*, many years later. Irma returned to Britain and went into partnership with Maggie Clegg at the corner shop, but she left for Llandudno in 1972 and

subsequently emigrated to Canada. It was a blow to the whole cast when Arthur Leslie, who played Jack Walker, died suddenly in 1970. The writers simply wrote Jack's death into the script, supposedly while visiting daughter Joan in Derbyshire, and widow Annie carried on, running the Rovers Return by herself. Anne Reid, who played Valerie Barlow, asked to leave the serial, so Ken's wife was written out with a fatal electric shock, courtesy of a faulty hairdrier plug.

Another real-life death that shocked the cast was that of Graham Haberfield, who played the nervous Jerry Booth. In 1975, he had a sudden heart attack and Jerry was written out with death from pneumonia. When actor Stephen Hancock wanted to leave in 1978, his character, Ernest Bishop, was fatally shot in a wages snatch at the warehouse. Ken Barlow married second wife Janet Reid (Judith Barker) in 1973, but they eventually split up and she committed suicide when she returned one night and slept on the sofa. Deirdre Hunt's marriage to Ray Langton finished when he started seeing waitress Janice Stubbs, then moved to Holland on a building contract, leaving Deirdre to look after daughter Tracy by herself. Divorce followed.

There were happier times for Len Fairclough and nightclub singer Rita Littlewood – played by Peter Adamson and Barbara Knox – after their 1977 wedding, but Elsie Tanner's marriage to Alan Howard, the *Street*'s first of the Seventies, was more stormy and they divorced in 1978. Pat Phoenix and Alan Browning, who played the couple, married in real life, but they suffered a similar fate. They left the *Street* in 1973 to concentrate on theatre, but Pat returned three years later. They had already split up when Alan died in 1979. Back in the *Street*, Gail Potter's marriage to Brian Tilsley was the last wedding of the Seventies and destined to have its own ups and downs.

Violet Carson, finding the strain of commuting from her Blackpool home too much, took a year's break, and some TV critics predicted that the exodus of characters would bring the *Street* to its knees. But a new set of screen favourites came to the fore, led by the fast-developing Ogdens – Stan and Hilda – great comedy favourites with more than a touch of Laurel and Hardy about their 'little and large' comic routines. Julie Goodyear and Betty Driver, as Bet Lynch and Betty Turpin, amply filled the gaps left at the Rovers Return and formed a comedy act of a different kind alongside Doris Speed, who played haughty Annie Walker.

When Maggie Clegg married reformed alcoholic Ron Cooke and left for Zaire, a whole new family – a rare occurrence in the programme – arrived at the corner shop in the shape of the Hopkins set, with *Last of the Summer Wine* star Kathy Staff among their ranks. Another family to arrive, in January 1979, were the Tilsleys – Ivy, Bert and grown-up son Brian. Former convict Eddie Yeats, superbly played by Geoffrey Hughes, became the *Street*'s No 1 prankster, taking over where another jailbird, Jed Stone, had left off.

▲ *Widowed Ken Barlow, running the community centre, begins a relationship with hotel receptionist Yvonne Chapel*

▼ *Gail Potter finds herself cited as co-respondent in a divorce case*

▲ *Stan and Hilda Ogden treat lodger Eddie Yeats like a son and he treats his landlady to a 'muriel' of the Alps*

► *Flighty Suzie Birchall demonstrates German sausage in the local supermarket*

▼ *The whole street get into the mood for the Queen's Silver Jubilee celebrations in 1977*

▲ *Stan Ogden offers Gail Potter and Suzie a ride on his tandem*

The Seventies was a prelude to the soap battles of the Eighties. On British television, *Coronation Street* and *Crossroads* were joined by *Emmerdale Farm*, a serial about rural life in the Yorkshire Dales, and this type of drama, focusing on people's everyday lives, was becoming an increasingly popular form of entertainment. But these programmes were exclusively British and the kitchen-sink drama was easy for viewers to relate to. As a new decade approached, the Americans would get in on the act, with glossy, escapist serials that were nothing short of fantasy, but totally compelling to millions. The challenge of those soaps and new British and Australian ones was to make *Coronation Street* fight its rivals and strive to even greater heights.

THE EIGHTIES

The Eighties was the decade of the soap opera. The shooting of J. R. Ewing in *Dallas* made newspaper headlines around the world in 1980 and triggered a tabloid newspaper obsession with soaps, although the word was redefined. Traditionally, soaps were half-hour serials screened more than once a week and for 52 weeks of the year. *Dallas* did not follow that formula, running 50 minutes weekly with seasonal breaks, but it and other serials were now called soaps, and newspapers and magazines vied to devote the greatest space to coverage of them.

New serials proliferated. *Dallas* was followed by *Dynasty* and they both had spin-offs. From Australia came *Neighbours* and *Home and Away*. At home, the new Channel Four introduced *Brookside*. Other newcomers failed, as did some long-established ones, notably *Crossroads*, originally started as a Midlands answer to the North's *Coronation Street*, which lurched to its end in 1988, after 24 years. Comparisons between the different productions, their stars and their

▲ *The* Street*'s Brat Pack: Stuart Wolfenden, Michelle Holmes, Sally Whittaker, Sally Ann Matthews, Michael Le Vell, Sean Wilson and, front, Kevin Kennedy*

audiences were drawn endlessly. They moved in and out of fashion.

What was to be called the war of the soaps began in earnest when the BBC launched *EastEnders* in 1985. The character of 'Dirty Den' Watts fascinated the tabloids and the serial went to the No 1 spot in the ratings, usurping the position traditionally held by *Coronation Street*. It was useless for Granada TV to point out that *EastEnders* had a weekend omnibus edition, which swelled the figures, or to protest that programme for programme the *Street* was still the more popular. The press showed *EastEnders* as No 1 in the ratings and, even though its audiences had not fallen, asked, 'Is *Coronation Street* on the skids?'

David Liddiment, executive producer of *Coronation Street*, says, 'If there isn't a war there isn't a story, and so there had to be an *EastEnders–Coronation Street* war. There had to be a rivalry, which was entirely derived from Fleet Street and didn't actually exist because the two programmes play on different days of the week.' But the tabloid insistence rankled. As Liddiment says, 'The great danger about being No 1 is that, when you're not No 1, you start to worry. Whatever we said about *EastEnders* and our popularity, the view persisted that we were ageing, decaying, declining and second-best. It was a view we never subscribed to, but which prevailed in the popular press, and it continued for several years, to a point where even fans of the programme were beginning to believe it.'

Eventually, the *Street* hit back with its own Sunday omnibus edition. It followed an experiment at the end of 1987, when the Christmas episode was repeated. It was a particularly poignant episode because it saw the departure of Jean Alexander as Hilda Ogden, a much loved character. The episode was Britain's most popular show that Christmas and, coupled with viewer research that showed that fans complained there was too big a gap between Wednesday and Monday episodes, helped Granada make the decision to start the omnibus in January 1989. *Coronation Street*'s Wednesday edition plus the Sunday repeat was seen by 22.9 million viewers, and the Monday edition plus Sunday repeat scored 21.5 million. The top figure from *EastEnders* was 18.7 million. 'It changed things,' says David Liddiment. 'I was rather surprised the press had believed their own hype, but we got the reverse benefit. All of a sudden, we were back on top, rejuvenated, No 1, and it was the other guys who were in trouble and having crisis talks. There's a tremendous charge from being back on top. It charged the cast and the production team and writers, and that gave us the confidence to go for the third episode.'

That development, one of the most significant in the serial's long history, came in October 1989. Granada's director of programmes Steve Morrison, still mindful of the viewer research, asked David Liddiment to look at the possibility of making a third weekly episode for Friday nights. There was an obvious risk in disturbing the viewing

▲ *Executive producer David Liddiment*

habits of a third of the population, and Friday had been for years a difficult and often low-rated night on ITV where other soaps had failed.

On the executive floor, there were doubts about whether the scriptwriters, actors and production team could prevent the lifeblood of the serial becoming thin with a 50 per cent increase in material. There were doubters even among the cast. Betty Driver, who plays Betty Turpin, confesses that she was one. 'I thought it was bound to be too much,' she says. And David Liddiment admits, 'I was very nervous. I didn't want to go down in the *Street*'s distinguished history as the man who killed the golden goose. We had already made the decision to increase the volume of location material and we were looking at a schedule to give us more time on location and the same time in the studio. I didn't want the process we'd started, of increasing the production values of an episode, to be neutralised by the need to make a third episode. I wanted to ensure we could continue to enhance the production values of the programme *and* do a third episode. But there was a kind of rhythm about Monday, Wednesday and Friday, and the fact that *Neighbours* and *Home and Away* were being shown five days a week with healthy audiences was, I felt, indicative of our ability to hold an audience for an extra episode.'

It was agreed to go ahead, and Steve Morrison offered Granada's proposal to the network. The network, seeing a possibility of strengthening its Friday schedules, 'snapped his hand off', to quote one executive. Leaving nothing to chance, the production team made sure that it had a strong storyline for the launch of the third episode. It centred on the return of Alan Bradley, who months earlier had been arrested after attempting to murder former lover Rita Fairclough. The Wednesday episode ended with him walking out of court a free man; the first Friday episode ended with him reappearing on Rita's doorstep. The success of the third episode exceeded the *Coronation Street* team's expectations. The *Street* took the top three places in the charts and was back in its accustomed place – unarguably. But no one at Granada has any ambition to expand to five episodes a week – they believe it could not be done without loss of quality.

In the Eighties, with the tabloids' obsession with soaps, *Coronation Street* made more headlines than ever before. The biggest sensation was probably Deirdre Barlow's havering between her husband and *Street* romeo Mike Baldwin, but there were others, including the Alan Bradley–Rita Fairclough saga, which ended when, pursuing the terrified Rita to Blackpool, he was hit by a tram and killed. There was also the on–off marriage of Brian and Gail Tilsley. The paternity of their daughter was in doubt after her adultery with his Australian cousin Ian Latimer, although it was established eventually that Sarah Louise was Brian's, but by then their marriage had broken up. They remarried and were estranged again, before Brian died, stabbed to death in an alley. Christopher Quinten, who played Brian, had fallen in love with an American

◀ Ken Barlow confronts wife Deirdre about her affair with Mike Baldwin and audience figures soar

▶ Gail Potter marries Brian Tilsley – for the first time – in 1979

▶ All together now! The men of the Rovers take on the Flying Horse regulars in the Pub Olympics

chat-show hostess and wanted to be written out so that he could join her in the US.

There were other departures. Ena Sharples made her last appearance in 1980, and the script had her moving to St Anne's-on-Sea. This was caused by the ill-health of Violet Carson, who played her in 1,148 episodes; she died in 1983. Elsie Tanner was written out when she went to Portugal to join old flame Bill Gregory. Pat Phoenix, who played her, left to look for other roles, and starred in the TV situation comedy *Constant Hot Water*, before her death in 1986. Bert Tilsley, Albert Tatlock and Stan Ogden all died in 1984, when Peter Dudley, Jack Howarth and Bernard 'Bunny' Youens, who played them, died. Len Fairclough and Renee Roberts, wife of Alf, died in road accidents. Chalkie Whiteley emigrated to Australia.

New characters came in, including Jill Summers as widowed Phyllis Pearce – setting her cap at busybody Percy Sugden (Bill Waddington) – man-hungry café owner Alma Sedgewick (Amanda Barrie) and town hall secretary Wendy Crozier (Roberta Kerr). Many newcomers were young: Michael Le Vell as garage mechanic Kevin Webster, and Sally Whittaker as Sally Seddon, who became his wife, Stuart Wolfenden as garage owner's son Mark Casey, Sally Ann Matthews as schoolgirl Jenny Bradley, and Sean Wilson as Martin Platt, her boyfriend for a time, Nigel Pavaro as Terry Duckworth, no-good son of Jack and Vera, and Kevin Kennedy as his egghead pal Curly Watts. Newspapers termed these, and the 14-year-old McDonald twins, introduced at Christmas 1989, the *Street*'s 'brat pack', and the serial was perceived as having a new appeal to young viewers, although it has always had youngsters in the cast, since Lucille Hewitt was its first moody teenager in 1960. 'We were losing a bit on the younger market,' admits David Liddiment. 'The *Street* had been around for 25 years and a lot of its audience had grown up with it. So I was conscious of the need to continue to appeal to the younger audience, but not necessarily by the injection of young people's stories because, if you do that, you alienate your older audiences. The last thing the *Street* should do is to start addressing the young specifically; it just wouldn't be appropriate. It is more truthful and effective to do as we

did in the story of Ken and Deirdre's separation, when we looked not just at these two characters but the impact on their 12-year-old daughter. I think that has broad appeal.'

There were marriages in the Eighties. Emily Bishop married Arnold Swain, but he was exposed as a bigamist and later died. Mike Baldwin, having had his way with Ken Barlow's wife Deirdre, married Ken's young daughter Susan, although they parted when she refused to have children. Other weddings included those of Fred Gee and Eunice Nuttall, Ken Barlow and Deirdre Langton, Alf Roberts and Audrey Potter, Eddie Yeats and Marion Willis, Kevin Webster and Sally Seddon, Alec Gilroy and Bet Lynch, Don Brennan and Ivy Tilsley, and Derek Wilton and Mavis Riley.

In the second half of the Eighties there were other new perceptions of *Coronation Street*. It was widely seen as sexier – or 'raunchier', as the press liked to say – with teenager Martin Platt becoming the 'toy boy' of widowed, nearing-40 Gail Tilsley, the adulterous Ken Barlow moving in with Wendy Crozier, who had leaked town hall secrets to his newspaper, and Curly Watts sharing a flat with Shirley Armitage. Some said they were shocked when they saw Gail and Martin or Ken and Wendy in bed together, although nobody had expressed shock when shown Stan Ogden and Hilda sharing a bed a decade earlier, but they, of course, were married.

'We show bedrooms more than we used to,' says David Liddiment, 'but I think, more than anything else, it is to do with the way we now make *Coronation Street*. In the last few years, we've transformed the way we make programmes. Up until a couple of years ago, each episode would probably have had no more than four or five different settings – either the shop or café and two or three interiors of houses, plus, at the most, two scenes shot outside on the street set or at a separate location. And each episode would have no more than 14 scenes. A typical episode now has eight or nine different interiors and four outside locations, and anything up to 22 or 23 scenes. We go more on location. We see more of Weatherfield than we used to do. We see more of the street. At one time, that wouldn't have happened because it was a luxury the schedule didn't allow, but we make TV now with lighter

▼ *Fred Gee threatens to sue Annie Walker when he falls down the cellar steps*

▶ *Bet Lynch, Rita Fairclough and Mavis Riley find a bit of holiday romance in Blackpool*

▲ *Kevin Webster and Terry Duckworth give Curly Watts some tips about girls*

▼ *It's a sad occasion for residents when Hilda leaves the street at Christmas 1987, after 23 years, to become Dr Lowther's housekeeper in Derbyshire. The Rovers regulars give her a good send-off*

equipment that requires less lighting, so we've got more time. Up to a few years ago, you couldn't have a bedroom because you couldn't fit it in the studio. The way we make the show now, if we need a bedroom we can have a bedroom. So bedroom scenes are probably as much to do with having a bedroom as anything to do with permissiveness.'

The most gripping story, which ran for eighteen months, was the Rita Fairclough–Alan Bradley saga. It began when Kabin papergirl Jenny Bradley's mother died and Rita decided to foster her. When Jenny's estranged father Alan arrived on the scene, his friendship with Rita grew to love and they were soon living together. Unlucky Rita's world was to be shattered when he walked out on her for another woman. Eventually, he returned, only to use the deeds of her house to obtain a loan for his own business. Almost twenty-seven million viewers saw the episode where she confronted him and

he tried to murder her. It was No 1 in the Eighties TV ratings, but more drama was to come. Alan was caught and held at Risley Remand Centre. He was convicted of fraud and assault – the police changed the charge from attempted murder – but released immediately because he had already spent seven months in detention. His pursuit of Rita ended when he was fatally hit by a Blackpool tram.

The Eighties also saw changes in the actual street. Alf Roberts converted the corner shop into a Mini Market, and the Rovers was rebuilt after being gutted by fire. As the decade ended, an even bigger change was the razing of Mike Baldwin's factory and the redevelopment of the site. David Liddiment had walked around Salford and seen terraced houses still existing but alongside little pockets of new developments, factory units and private housing. That was one factor. Another practical one was that the outside

▲ *Fred Gee drives Bet and Betty to the park. The car rolls into the lake*

▼ *A miscarriage saddens Alec and Bet Gilroy, who each already have a 'secret' child*

▼ *A comforting hand comes from Martin Platt as Jenny Bradley grieves her father's sudden death*

location of the existing street restricted camera angles. Redeveloping one side would give more flexibility. Viewers saw it happen over a six-month period, during which stories of Baldwin's financial affairs and the builders working on the site were woven in.

So, as the serial moved into the Nineties, there was a new street and, although the seven terraced houses were retained, there was an opportunity to bring in new characters and move some of the established characters who lived elsewhere into the street itself. Some saw this as the 'yuppification' of the street. Certainly, characters are more prosperous than when *Coronation Street* began, and they rented their homes from a landlord named Wormald. Today, most of them own their own. They dine out. Vera Duckworth runs a car. But, then, many real-life Coronation Streets have also become more prosperous. There are, as yet, no yuppies with Porsches. Nor are there

likely to be, although more changes can be expected.

'It was characterised a few years ago as a serial which lived in its own world, caught in its own kind of time warp,' says David Liddiment. 'A detailed analysis of the programme doesn't quite bear that out. It's changed dramatically through its thirty years. It's never stopped changing and we wouldn't be on the air now, in my view, if it hadn't changed and evolved and, if it doesn't keep on evolving, it will die. From time to time, we need an injection of new characters to stir things up a bit. From time to time, we need to address in a fundamental way some of our longer-running characters and shake them up a bit. The characters become more fascinating the more you mix them. But, if we make changes, we make them with great respect. There is an obligation to keep it refreshed and alert, but you can't radicalise it, can't make it into something else.'

▲ *Gail and Brian Tilsley are the proud parents watching on as son Nicky is christened*

▼ *Vera Duckworth tackles Rovers barmaid Tina Fowler over her night on the town with Jack*

THE PRODUCER'S VIEW

▲ *Mervyn Watson produces the programme that regularly holds the top three spots in the TV ratings*

When Mervyn Watson first worked on *Coronation Street*, in 1983, it was his first assignment as a producer. He was inexperienced and very nervous. 'Over those two-and-a-half years, anything that could happen *did* happen,' he recalls. 'It was as if everything had waited for this novice to arrive and then blew up. Pat Phoenix left and Jack Howarth, Peter Dudley and Bernard Youens all, sadly, died. Peter Adamson was acquitted of headline-making charges and not one weekend passed without another sensational set of stories blazed across the Sunday papers. And, within the programme, the great Ken–Mike–Deirdre epic scorched across our screens. Amazing times.'

Mervyn returned to the *Street* in December 1988 and, during the following year, saw some of the most profound changes in the programme's history. An omnibus edition, three episodes a week, and Baldwin's factory demolished and replaced by houses. 'Our new Friday episode has often had the highest audience of the week,' says Mervyn, 'and we regularly hold the top three places in the national Top 10 programmes. Also, the reconstruction of the even-numbers side of the street has opened up a whole new swathe of stories and characters. It was appropriate that the first occupants of No 6 Coronation Street should be newcomers, the hot-tempered newlyweds Des and Steph Barnes. By mixing old and new, our well established characters have been given new possibilities and a new lease of life.'

Life has, of course, changed for those making the programme. Fifty per cent more episodes each week actually means about seventy per cent more work, so more production staff have been employed: a programme manager, two unit managers to supervise exterior recording, and more secretaries. Four directors are making or planning programmes at any one time and the storyline department has been increased from two to three people, mapping out the events that will be turned into scripts. 'Life is much harder and faster than it was,' says Mervyn, 'and one thing is certain – we can't make more than three episodes a week!

'When I came back to the *Street*, I felt that the programme needed gee-ing up slightly, so I encouraged more stories every week and more scenes in each episode, thereby increasing the pace slightly. And the stories have been cracking! We've had the tragic murder of Brian Tilsley, Alan Bradley's sensational fraud, attempted murder, trial and sudden death, Rita Fairclough's stoic triumph in the face of that, Ken Barlow's affair with Wendy Crozier, Mike Baldwin's financial ruin, and the threat to Bet Gilroy by Alec's search for his long-lost daughter. On the lighter side, there's been Jack Duckworth struggling to come to terms with middle-age, failing powers and spectacles, Derek talking himself out of a job and into the funny-nose business, then having a final run-in with his rival for Mavis's affections, Victor Pendlebury, only to become manager of his company, and Alf and Audrey Roberts's lost new home. Comic or dramatic, they were all terrific stories.

'Whatever we can or can't do, we'll always be knocked by some viewers and critics, from diametrically opposite positions, either for not being up-to-date enough or for being too up-to-date. The truth is that the programme is constantly updating itself while maintaining its traditional values. While the amount of story has increased and the "world" of *Coronation Street* has enlarged as we go out and about with our new lightweight cameras, the *people*, and the way they deal with each other, retain their character, strength, warmth and humour. When the *Street* first hit the screens in 1960, its impact derived from the honest representation of working-class people and their lives. A lot has changed, but that representation retains its original honesty and commitment, so *Coronation Street* remains true and constant.'

William Roache

KEN BARLOW

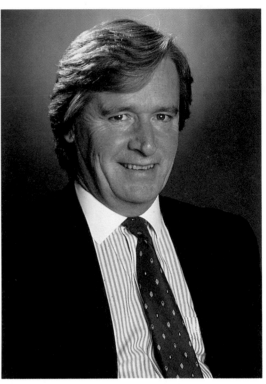

William Roache is the only surviving member of the cast who appeared in *Coronation Street*'s first episode. He describes his character as 'a one-man Greek tragedy', having lost both his parents, his brother, nephew and two wives. His third wife, of course, threw him out over his affair with Wendy Crozier.

Ken Barlow began as a bit of a prig, in the eyes of his working-class father Frank, but matured into a sound, family man, only to go astray. He changed from teacher to newspaper owner, through various jobs, but

▲ *Jack Walker consoles Ken and father Frank after Ida Barlow's tragic death, hit by a bus*

threw that away, too. He has always liked to see himself as a big fish in a small pond, with his steely, domineering manner and feeling of superior intellect.

Thankfully, William's own life has not had so many ups and downs. Born in Ilkeston, Derbyshire, a doctor's son, he was educated at Rydal School, in North Wales, and gave up medicine for a regular commission in the Royal Welsh Fusiliers. He served in Jamaica, British Guiana, Bermuda, Germany and then, for two years, in Arabia, where he worked with Bedouin tribesmen and 'went native', living as an Arab and even riding camels. Years later, when the late Eamonn Andrews went to Manchester to surprise William with the famous *This Is Your Life* book, he appeared in flowing robes with spitting camel, recalling the *Street* star's Lawrence of Arabia act.

In Arabia, William was the only Briton among 125 non-English-speaking Arabs and was called upon to settle tribal disputes – 'of which there were plenty,' he recalls. 'I enjoyed my five years in the Army but realised that it was not what I really wanted out of life. I resigned my commission and decided to give acting a try, eventually winning a small part in the Michael Redgrave film *Behind the Mask.*' After appearing in repertory theatre in Clacton, Nottingham and Oldham, he landed TV roles in the Granada series *Knight Errant* and *Skyport,* in which Doris Speed – who was to play Rovers Return landlady Annie Walker – once pushed a tea trolley, and the film *Bulldog Breed.*

A devoted family man, William and actress wife Sara live in Cheshire with their children, Verity and William, who both have famous *Coronation Street* godmothers. Eileen Derbyshire, who plays Emily Bishop, is godmother to Verity, and Betty Driver, who plays Betty Turpin, is William's godmother. Betty was also godmother to the Roaches' second daughter, Edwina, who tragically died of a sudden viral attack when she was just eighteen months old. 'My family is the single most important thing in my life,' says William, 'and our average day is so hectic that I am reduced to doing my thinking in the smallest room in the house. Sara and I have a very full life with the children,' says William. 'Having youngsters at my time of life certainly keeps me young. I'm not quite as physically capable as I was, but, mentally and

emotionally, I feel like a twenty-year-old. Ken is ten years younger than me, so he keeps me fit, too.' He also has a son, Linus, and daughter, Vanya, by his first marriage, to actress Anna Cropper.

William, who is a director of Lancashire Cable Television and has connections with the independent local radio station Red Rose, is intensely proud of both *Coronation Street* and Ken Barlow. 'He is a man of integrity who fights for what he thinks is right,' he says. 'For my part, if there is an injustice done to Ken, I will fight on his behalf. I regard myself as Ken's caretaker.'

Ken was brought up on a diet of ding-dong rows, first with father Frank and then with tetchy 'Uncle' Albert. Then, he had to fight to save his marriage to Deirdre when she had an affair with Mike Baldwin, but six years later embarked on his own extra-marital relationship with Wendy Crozier. Heavy, drama-laden scenes have been Ken's lot over the years.

'It still excites me, after thirty years,' says William, 'and I look forward with great interest to what is happening in the storyline. I still want to learn as an actor and still want to manoeuvre the character into a more exciting position.

'It'll be my thirtieth anniversary, too, on 9 December 1990 – something of which I am very proud of having achieved. I wouldn't like anyone to think I have just coasted along in the programme. *Coronation Street* feeds beautifully any acting beast I have in me. I recognise the wonderful work being done in theatre, but I don't enjoy stage work myself any more. I prefer the intimacy of television. I would like to develop as a writer, possibly, and I suppose the other thing I would like to do before I die is a big feature film. It would be nice to leave the *Street* on loan, so to speak, then come back.

'Overall, I like to think that we are a nice programme that purveys good quality. We combine comedy with community spirit and social realism. We have always been slightly behind the times, but that is the nature of the show – it isn't a criticism to say that. There is a slightly nostalgic feel about *Coronation Street*. I always used to love "Uncle" Albert clanking in with his World War One medals and all the wonderful, little chats you could have about that era. We have a dignity that a lot of other soaps lack.'

Eileen Derbyshire

EMILY BISHOP

If Eileen Derbyshire had her way, she would be working in the great Edwardian theatre era, in which actresses would melt into the night in a flurry of ostrich feathers, leaving an aura of mystery behind them at the stage door. Eileen dislikes publicity and is loath to talk about her personal life. She thinks it a great pity that the media peer so closely into actors' lives, destroying the mystique of the characters they play. 'It ruins the illusion actors try to create,' says the Manchester-born actress known to millions as Emily Bishop, who has been one of the great cornerstones of *Coronation Street* since Episode Three in January 1961.

Born in Manchester, she married a local businessman, Tom, in 1965, and they have a 22-year-old son Oliver, who read history at Oxford University. Eileen's 90-year-old mother lives with them in the Cheshire countryside. Their social life is muted. 'I'm not a party person,' says Eileen. 'If I have eight friends to dinner, that's the limit. I want to be able to hear the conversation clearly and talk to everyone in the room, including the most interesting person.'

Eileen loves the arts, with a special passion for literature, opera and art exhibitions. 'We love Italy particularly and have travelled extensively to Florence, Rome, Venice and the Italian lakes,' she says. 'I'm a great book person – I call myself a printoholic. Without something to read, I think I'd go mad.'

Eileen was tied up in a Christmas stage play in December 1960 when Granada first approached her about *Coronation Street.* 'Four weeks after it started, they said I could either wait until they introduced a new family into the programme or take the tiny part of a little, shy woman helper at the Mission Hall,'

says Eileen. 'I have always been a fatalist, so I took the bird in the hand, not realising what a momentous decision I was making.'

Public recognition is something Eileen tolerates quietly and with good humour. 'It's still difficult to shop in public without a fuss,' she says, 'but it's something you just have to get used to. 'What worries me slightly is that some people really think I am Emily, and they will make assumptions. They'll apologise for swearing, or say, "Oh, you don't take a drink, do you?" as if they know your personal habits. I often feel like the members of those primitive tribes who don't like their photographs taken because they feel part of their soul is being taken away. Life is too short to explain to that person the whole concept of acting or that you are totally different from the character.'

Eileen has fond memories of the early days of *Coronation Street,* playing opposite Arthur Lowe, before he left eventually to star in *Dad's Army.* 'In a way, we laid the foundations for what is happening today,' she says. 'The show was fresh and new. I hate to say it but, whereas it is built up of celebrities today, we had more of a team spirit going. There was a special bond between us be-

cause the programme was done live and it was jolly hard work. We were experiencing everything for the first time, from the sort of mob receptions in public reserved for pop stars to the tragic death of Arthur Leslie [Jack Walker], the first member of the cast to die. It hit us all very hard.'

The programme can go on and on, Eileen believes, 'if it stays gentle. I know we have to reflect changes in moral behaviour, but there are limits. I would not be happy appearing in a programme full of sex, violence and bad language that had no justification for being there. The cast are closer to public reaction than anybody and it's amazing how contented people are just to hear about and discuss the most trivial aspects of a storyline or a character. If we change the wallpaper or the cushion covers, they'll say, "My mother used to have something similar in the lounge." They don't want sensation. Gratuitous violence, particularly, has no place in a serial like ours.'

For an opinionated actress, she has no strong feelings about what fate should befall Emily in terms of, for instance, marriage. 'The writers have a tough enough task as it is, trying to find new storylines for a charac-

ter who has been in the serial for three decades,' she says. 'I just get on with it. Emily has had a more colourful past than you might think. She has had lots of men friends and liaisons. In the early days, when they were stuck for something to do with her, I think the writers used to say, "Let's give Emily another boyfriend." I've lost count of the number of men friends she has had.'

Recently, perky pensioner Percy Sugden – actor Bill Waddington – who moved in as her lodger, has had romantic designs on the long-suffering Emily. In 1989, romance appeared to blossom with Arthur Dabner (Michael Sheard), who was separated from his wife Babs, but he decided to give his marriage another chance.

'In the middle years, I did miss Arthur Lowe terribly,' says Eileen. 'We had such a good screen relationship going for us and he was a lovely man, too. Now, I feel I might have found the same chemical mix with Bill Waddington. Emily needs other characters to bounce off, and Percy is wonderful.

'The difference between me and the character? She is a little too straitlaced and lacking in humour, but she does have integrity and the courage of her convictions.'

Anne Kirkbride

AS
DEIRDRE BARLOW

Anne Kirkbride has known nothing but *Coronation Street* since she left Oldham Rep at the age of 18. Like many members of the serial's cast, she trained at Oldham, starting as an assistant stage manager, before getting the chance to act. When she joined the *Street* in 1972, she had already been in a Granada TV play, *Another Sunday and Sweet FA*, about what happened when the Co-op Albion's Second Eleven clashed with Parker Street Bus Depot. Anne was seen standing on a windy touchline, wearing hot-pants and a yellow bob-cap. Then she auditioned for the 'pilot' of a new series and a casting director offered her a bit part in *Coronation Street*. It required just three lines when Elsie Tanner walked into a pub and found then husband Alan Howard drinking with Deirdre Hunt. 'She wasn't pleased,'

says Anne. 'That was my first *Street* episode and I was petrified at the thought of coming into something I'd been watching since the age of seven.'

The Mike–Ken–Deirdre saga, in 1983, had an impact that Anne had not expected. 'It was simply unbelievable at the time,' she said. 'I thought the story would spark off a few fan letters, but I never imagined anything like the press and public reaction we got. It was great stuff – the sort of thing you only get to play once a decade, but I never dreamed it would grip the nation like it did. It was scary. Fortunately, I was working all the time, so I just kept my head down and got on with it. I can't say I enjoyed the experience. I enjoyed the work, but it's the rest of it I can't handle.'

The unexpected was also sprung on Anne while recording the scene where Mike confronted Ken and Deirdre on their doorstep. 'Deirdre told him that Ken knew about them,' Anne recalls. 'Then, Ken slammed the door, shoved me against the wall and went for my throat. It was quite frightening and I hadn't expected it. He had worked it out with the director, Brian Mills, so that it was totally realistic. I was very upset at the time and just ran into the living room and sat down with my head in my hands – and Brian had a camera there, waiting to film me!'

Away from the studios, Anne is everything that Deirdre is not. Dubbed 'Sexy Specs' by some newspapers, she actually wears contact lenses and prefers jeans to Deirdre's pinnie, and enjoys pottering around in her garden. 'The *Street* is like any job,' she says. 'It has its good days and bad days. I just enjoy having something to do that's good, something that's interesting and gives me a lot of scope. I wouldn't be here if I wanted to perform Shakespeare. I never really wanted to be an actress. It's a nine-to-five job. This is how I earn my money. Half my life has been spent in this show and it's made me the sort of person I am. When I'm away from it, I lead as normal a life as people will let me. The thought of this show coming off or me losing my job fills me with terror.'

Johnny Briggs

AS

MIKE BALDWIN

Battersea-born Johnny Briggs began his long showbusiness career as a boy soprano. At the age of twelve, he won a scholarship at the famous Italia Conti stage school. 'I quickly found myself in the chorus of an Italian opera company, singing in *La Bohème*, *Tosca* and *Rigoletto*,' says Johnny.

Later, in the chorus of a revue called *Sauce Tartare*, he danced with Audrey Hepburn. In terms of major credits, Johnny has been around more than most, with over fifty feature films to his name, including *Hue and Cry*, *HMS Defiant*, *Doctor In Love*, and several *Carry On . . .* films.

He came from a talented bunch of young actors that included Millicent Martin, Nanette Newman and Anthony Newley. Other pals and associates who went on to become famous included Sean Connery, Peter O'Toole and Michael Caine. Rank

starlet Joan Collins appeared with Johnny in the 1952 film *Coshboy*. 'I was 17 and played a character called Skinny, and she was 19 and played the gang-leader's girlfriend,' recalls Johnny. 'She was a pretty girl then, but rather plumpish. In my opinion, she looks a good deal more glamorous now.'

His TV career began in the North in 1960, when he appeared in a series called *The Younger Generation*, with John Thaw and Judy Cornwell. Since then, he has been in many television series, including *Z-Cars*, *The Avengers*, *Crossroads*, *The Saint*, *Danger Man* and the top-rated ITV crime programme *No Hiding Place*, in which he played Det Sgt Russell. In 1973, he was offered the part of Clifford Leyton, a taxi fleet owner, in *Crossroads* – his first taste of soap. 'I didn't enjoy it much because I hadn't seen the programme and didn't realise it wasn't quite my style.' Three years later, he made his debut in the *Street* as the pushy cockney factory boss Mike Baldwin, brought into the Northern soap to help improve ratings in London and the south.

In his private life, too, Johnny has abandoned his London roots. Home is Stourbridge, Worcestershire, where he lives with his schoolteacher wife Christine and their four children, Jennifer Louise, Michael Lawrence, Stephanie Elizabeth and Anthony Stacey.

During the week, he lives in a bachelor flat at the renovated Manchester dockland site of Salford Quays. 'I'm just like Mike Baldwin,' says Johnny. 'I've got bottles of wine in the fridge and I can just about manage to cook a fillet steak. After that, I've had it.' So, on Friday nights, he drives down to Stourbridge in his Jaguar saloon and takes his dirty washing with him. Away from the studios, his hobbies are golf and raising money for charity. 'Luckily, I can very often combine the two in showbiz tournaments,' says Johnny. He stopped playing squash, he says dryly, 'when my wife started to beat me'.

Professionally, he is one of the most unpretentious actors around. 'I don't really go into work all that deeply,' says Johnny. 'I just get on with it. I don't act in *Coronation Street* all that much. To me, acting is something you do when you're doing Shakespeare. I only did that once and I hated it. I am a jobbing actor – I get on with the job and, as a result, have always worked.'

Julie Goodyear

A S
BET GILROY

▼ *Since her first days in the Rovers as a dollybird barmaid, Bet has pulled in the customers*

W hen Bet Lynch started working as a barmaid at the Rovers Return 20 years ago, landlady Annie Walker regarded her as common but soon realised that the blonde hair, ample bosom and quickfire banter pulled in the customers. She has had more than her fair share of knocks but always picks herself up off the floor. Now, she has finally found happiness with Alec Gilroy. It was largely a marriage of convenience when they wed in 1987, but they have made it an undoubted success.

Julie Goodyear's own romances have been less happy. Married and divorced three times, she is now resolved not to marry again. 'I don't think it will happen,' she says. 'Three times unlucky is enough.' Pregnant with son Gary, she married Ray Sutcliffe while still in her teens, but within three years they had split up. Later, she wed businessman Tony Rudman, who walked out on her

at the wedding reception. Then, in 1985, she married American businessman Richard Skrob, but they were divorced two years later.

'I don't feel I've ever been married,' says Julie. 'There were quite long gaps in between. The first time, I was 17 and pregnant. We were both too young. I was 29 the next time, and I think the enormous popularity of the character I played was a tremendous shock to my husband on the actual wedding day. We had really just gone out together very quietly and privately while we were engaged, but fans turned up in their thousands at the wedding. The impact of that probably had a great deal to do with what happened.

'It was more than ten years before I got married again. It's not something you're thinking about when you are busy working. We met on a plane when I was travelling to New Zealand to promote *Coronation Street*.

We kept in touch, married and, sadly, that didn't work. The distance between us became too wide. He had business in America but had always said that he would be moving nearer. But, after two years, I realised that if he hadn't moved by then, he wasn't going to. I bear no ill will or bitterness to any of my husbands. I sincerely hope they are happy.'

More trauma came for Julie after a routine check for cervical cancer in 1979 showed that she needed surgery. After undergoing two operations, she was given the all-clear. 'I was very fortunate, very lucky indeed,' she reflects now. But her brush with cancer was to lead to an unexpected brush with the law, as a result of the charity fund she set up with the aim of starting a laboratory to detect cervical cancer. She was charged with defrauding the fund but was acquitted after the judge directed the jury to find her and two other defendants not guilty. 'It was one of the worst times of my life,' says Julie. 'I was working on *Coronation Street* for a year while on bail and I had to stand in Manchester Crown Court for five days before the judge completely threw out the case. In retrospect, if you lend your name to something like that, you have to be prepared for things you would never expect to happen. Something had been going wrong with a section of the charity that I knew nothing about, the sale of raffle tickets, and it's impossible to know about every ticket being sold.

'I had to decide whether to continue because the lab wasn't built. My mother begged me to forget it completely – understandably, after watching her daughter go through a year of hell. I decided to see the job through. Bet would probably have done that.'

Julie's mother later suffered terminal cancer and, in 1987, the much-loved actress took a prolonged break from *Coronation Street* to nurse the tiny woman she loved deeply through her final months. Today, the Julie Goodyear Laboratory, at the Christie Hospital, Manchester, analyses all smear tests taking place in the North West. 'Originally, I wanted to track smear tests back to know where they went,' says Julie. 'I found a collection of Nissen huts that people were trying to function in, in poor conditions, so I decided to do something about it. I'm very proud of the laboratory and the medical team.'

Julie's pride in the laboratory is matched only by that of being a member of the *Coronation Street* cast, an ambition she held since the programme's start in 1960. 'I gave birth to my son, Gary, the same year that Tony Warren gave birth to *Coronation Street*,' she says. 'I watched it from the beginning and knew it was for me.'

Her father was a publican, keeping the Bay Horse in Heywood, Lancashire, for 13 years. Julie served behind the bar there only twice and both times there was a fight, with her in it. Julie's original ambition was to be a singer, but she soon decided that acting was for her. She brought up son Gary single-

▼ *Bet and Alec Gilroy's marriage of convenience turned to real love*

handed, did office work to support him and managed to save up for a modelling course, which eventually led to television work. Between acting jobs, she sold household appliances door-to-door.

Without any formal drama training, Julie landed the role of Bet Lynch, one of the girls in *Coronation Street*'s raincoat factory, in 1966. 'They sussed me out and chucked me out,' she says. 'I was furious. Pat Phoenix advised me to train in repertory theatre and I did 12 months at Oldham Rep, then came back and they didn't want me. I was absolutely crushed. I wanted the *Street*, nothing else, but I stuck to Granada just to show them I could do different things. I was in *The Dustbinmen*, *The War of Darkie Pilbeam* and *Nearest and Dearest*. Then, June Howson was directing *A Family at War* and was about to take over as producer of *Coronation Street*. I did a small cameo part in *A Family at War* and, when I finished, she asked if I would be interested in being a regular member of the cast of *Coronation Street*. I couldn't believe it. I thought she was sending me up or kidding, and I didn't believe it until I got a contract.'

The *Street*'s professionalism and quality mean a lot to Julie. 'If the standard ever went down, I would leave,' she says. 'I would be absolutely mortified if it went down like *Crossroads* did and turned into a joke.

'All of us in the cast are very demanding of each other. Yes, I'm difficult. Anybody who admits to being a perfectionist in their work is bound to be difficult. I'm very demanding of other departments around me – make-up, costume, props, lighting. I tell them if I think something isn't quite right. I expect them to work as hard as I do. I go back to my dressing-room before going into the studio and look in the full-length mirror and I know if everything is right. If it's not, I go back to make-up or costume and say I think we need this or that. Then I check the Rovers set before I use it, even down to a last beer mat. I check that all the pumps and the tills are working, and check what flowers are on the bar and that the flowers on the top of the piano are in the right position, that there are enough mixer drinks, and that the glasses I'm going to be using to serve cast and "extras" are clean.'

As *Coronation Street*'s best-loved star, Julie has had to cope with the press following

▲ *Bet is a wow in Majorca, 1974*

every aspect of her life, and now chooses not to give interviews. 'They fantasise about me to such an extent that it's not necessary,' she says. 'If I did speak to them, they would be terribly disappointed because I'm very boring compared with the legend they have created. I've been offered £100,000 to give a one-word reply and turned that down. If, one day, certain levels of the British press behave in a different manner, then they will find me reacting very differently. While they continue to earn their reputation as the gutter press there's no way I will have anything to do with them. Abroad, it's different. The press in Canada, New Zealand and Australia are charming, well mannered, polite and ask intelligent questions. They also make appointments – they don't know what door-stepping means.'

Wherever she goes, Julie has time for her adoring fans. 'People come up to me and put their arms around me,' she says. 'I always get cuddles and hugs. It's been like that ever since I've played Bet.'

Betty Driver

AS
BETTY TURPIN

Betty Driver was actually working behind a bar when she was invited to play barmaid Betty Turpin. She was licensee of The Cock at Whaley Bridge, on the Cheshire–Derbyshire border, when *Coronation Street* producer Harry Kershaw visited her in 1969 and said, 'Come and pull pints in the *Street*.' 'Perhaps,' she says, 'that's why I feel so much at home playing Betty Turpin. It's been twenty years. Amazing! It seems like six months.'

Not that she was long a publican in real life. Betty had enjoyed a successful career as a singer, but it was ended by illness. 'I worked throughout my life, from nine or ten, and never had time off, and when I started there weren't the microphones there are now,' she says. 'I damaged my throat, got corns on the back of it and had to have them removed, and it took my singing voice away.'

Born in Leicester, Betty moved to Manchester with her family when she was two. A few years later, she started her career in variety and played all over the country. At the age of twelve, she went into radio and, in the Forties, sang with bandleader Henry Hall, made records, travelled the world to entertain the troops, did her own show in

Australia, and acted in Ealing comedy films and two London West End shows. Later, she starred in two musical shows on television, then played a bossy canteen manageress in the comedy series *Pardon the Expression*. Her other work included radio plays, her own series called *A Date With Betty* and cabaret work in Cyprus, Malta and the Middle East. She married South African singer Walley Petersen, but they separated seven years later and subsequently divorced.

Ask her which has been the most satisfying part of her life – as a singer or actress – and she plumps without hesitation for singing. 'I've always been a singer and was top of the bill wherever I sang all over the world. My next loveliest time has been in *Coronation Street*, because I never liked being in variety. My mother loved it and I was forced to sing and be in variety when I was a little girl and I just carried on from there.'

Betty lives in Cheshire with her sister, two boxer dogs and a cat called Abby – short for Absalom. She relaxes by pottering in the garden and greenhouse. 'I love plants and trees and flowers, and our house is always full of pot plants,' she says. 'Life without plants and flowers would be empty for me.' She does no acting outside *Coronation Street*. 'I don't have the enthusiasm,' she says. 'I let the others do that. When I have time off, my sister and I go round ancestral homes and we love the countryside. I feel very strongly about the countryside and nature. I think we're crucifying this fantastic planet. It's obviously going the way of other planets, which burned themselves up. It's very worrying. I'm old, but I do worry about the future for young people with babies.

'I like meeting people, and there are a lot of young ones in the *Street* today. It's noisy now! They wear you out sometimes. But they're all lovely, a joy to be with. *Coronation Street* used to have a middle-aged cast. This injection of youth is marvellous. I shall never quit – they'll have to shoot me! I don't want my brain to go *yuk*. I want to keep alert. I know so many who get to retiring age and just sit in a chair and that's that. I've no intention of packing it in.'

Roy Barraclough

ALEC GILROY

Some actors pop up in the *Street* playing more than one part, but veteran comic actor Roy Barraclough holds the record – he has played five characters. The last of them, Alec Gilroy, first appeared in the Seventies, as Rita Fairclough's theatrical agent. When he returned in 1986, it was as manager of the Graffiti Club, at the end of Coronation Street. Alec lent Bet Lynch money to buy the tenancy of the Rovers Return and when she disappeared, he tracked her down in Spain, where she was waitressing, and proposed marriage. That way, the brewery Newton and Ridley would give him the tenancy and Bet could still be landlady. The wedding went ahead and the partnership, personal and professional, has worked out. He has a streak of meanness with money and occasionally disappears on tour with his dubious theatrical acts, but the marriage suits them both.

'Alec started off very much harder,' recalls Roy. 'I think that hardness is still lurking there, waiting to get out. It's only Bet who manages to suppress it. I hope that hard, shrewd businessman side of him is allowed to come out from time to time. They've developed it into him being very mean, which I think is a rather cheap comedy device, although it makes for good banter with Bet. I personally enjoy playing comedy and I suppose you couldn't have him too evil in the Rovers. Running the pub, it's important that viewers can sympathise with him and see him as a lovable rogue.

'He was very much taken with Bet, and marriage has changed him. At the time it was suggested, it was a shock, not least to Julie Goodyear and me. I was a bit worried because, when people get married in the *Street*, they sometimes lose a bit of the grit. For Alec, in that seedy little area, Bet represented showbusiness. She was the only one around there with style, panache, theatricality. Julie and I have worked very hard at making the two characters work as a couple, but we already knew each other so well. I performed at Oldham Rep more than 20 years ago when she was an assistant stage manager there and we've always been good friends and had a natural rapport and share the same, rather bizarre sense of humour. We have a lot of fun in rehearsals and joke a lot, which leads to a very relaxed atmosphere.'

Preston-born Roy's first big break in showbusiness came when he became a 'feed' to fellow-Lancashire comedian Les Dawson on TV and they created Cissie and Ada, two old gossips. Roy also starred in a children's TV series, *Pardon My Genie*, and has made numerous other screen appearances.

'My first love is theatre,' says Roy, 'and I do get very itchy feet to get back on the stage again. On the other hand, Granada are quite good and they allow me eight weeks out in a year to do a play. That helps enormously. For the foreseeable future, I will continue playing Alec because I'm enjoying it, but two years ago I thought I was going to pack it all in. The actor's instinct is to do something and, having done it and achieved it, move on and tackle another challenge. With soap, once you have established the character, it's just a case of learning a different situation each week. There's nothing else to explore. But Granada outlined all sorts of interesting ideas they had to develop the character and it sounded smashing.'

Roy has his own theories about the reasons for *Coronation Street*'s long-running success. 'It's had peaks and troughs, as one would expect,' he says, 'but, overall, it has maintained a very high standard of writing and acting. That's a good basis for any successful programme. I always think it's a nice, safe show that people can sit down and watch as a family, without worrying that the kids are going to be exposed to bad language or undue violence. It's really family entertainment. I don't think it should be harder.

They've gently updated it, but they haven't done anything very drastic. It would be a disaster to do so. Otherwise, you end up with the *EastEnders* scenario – they shot all their big bolts and had nowhere to go.'

The change from two to three episodes a week has made great demands on the cast. 'It's damned hard work,' says Roy. 'If you're featured prominently in a storyline for five or six weeks, the pressure begins to get to you and the strain really starts to tell. It's very much bed and work. At the moment it's OK, but one could foresee a time when it could all get too much. I spend my life permanently tense.

'I'm a very private person and I tend to shun publicity. An actor is really an observer of life and people. To be an observer, you should be in the background, and I don't subscribe to all the business of the public knowing all about you and that you have three boiled eggs and All Bran for breakfast.

▲ *Roy Barraclough loves playing comedy roles, so his quickfire banter with Julie Goodyear behind the bar of the Rovers ensures fun on screen*

That shouldn't be of any concern to the public. All the actor owes the public is a bloody good performance. But I don't mind the intrusion into my private life from people asking for autographs in a restaurant. I enjoy meeting and talking to people, and little old ladies used to poke me in the back with umbrellas in the early days in the *Street*.'

One secret he does let out is that Alec's tipple, Irish whiskey, is not for him. 'I used to drink Scotch,' he says, 'until I had a rather unfortunate experience a couple of years ago. I got so drunk and was so ill that I've never been able to face it since. I now drink only gin and tonics. Oh, and the whiskey you see Alec drinking is really apple juice!'

Bryan Mosley

AS

ALF ROBERTS

Alf Roberts is known to residents of Coronation Street as owner of the corner shop, but actor Bryan Mosley believes he keeps the secret of a background that helped to form the character who has become a pillar of the community. 'There's a lot in him that's not been explored on screen,' says Bryan. 'There's something of a fighter in Alf. He was in the army during the war and probably had quite a difficult war. He's still interested in the weapons of the 1940s. All that has been glossed over. Part of the way I play him is that he has this experience behind the staid image. He has been to strip clubs with Ray Langton and Ernest Bishop, and he had a girlfriend called Donna Parker that no one in the *Street*, only viewers, knew.'

Bryan has also been a bit of a fighter himself. He was a stunt arranger and fight choreographer who helped to found the Society of British Fight Directors.' I did quite a lot of that. It kept the wolf from the door. I can still fence, but the last fight I had was with Ian Hendry in *The High Game*, for Anglia TV in the 1960s.'

Leeds-born Bryan has been in TV programmes such as *Z-Cars*, *Armchair Theatre*, *The Avengers* and *Doctor Who*, and the films *A Kind of Loving*, *Charlie Bubbles* and *Far From the Madding Crowd*. He joined *Coronation Street* in 1961 as Alf Roberts, a friend of Ken Barlow's postman father Frank. An actors' union strike towards the end of the year meant that Bryan and other cast members not on long-term contracts had to leave. 'In 1968, they asked me if I'd like to come back for a few months and I've been here ever since,' he says.

'I don't go along with Alf about a lot of things. I don't spend time in pubs – it's a tremendous waste of time. He has a very limited outlook on travel and is never seen to read. I'm sure he does – he probably reads Tolstoy, but it's never been shown. I've got my own secret world of Alf that I work from.'

Bryan's saddest memory from the *Street* was when actor Graham Haberfield, who played Jerry Booth, died suddenly in 1975. 'The day Graham died was a terrible time,' he recalls. 'It's always particularly hard when you work with someone constantly. Graham was only 34 and a great actor. I did a scene with Graham when Alf's first wife died and he went round to see Len, but only Jerry was there and Alf broke down. Graham and I were both emotional about that.'

Away from the studios, Bryan is married with six children and five grandchildren. He and wife Norma live in his native Yorkshire, and his three sons and daughter all work in the theatre. 'It's just part of their lives. They always had actors staying at the house, quite well-known ones at times. They were real people to them, not stars.'

Bryan also takes a paternal interest in the future of his screen 'family'. 'We've been through ups and downs,' he says, 'but there's so much energy about now and such talent, with some of the new cast members coming in and some of the old ones still here. I've changed during my years in the *Street*. I'm less worried about things. My wife was very ill and got over it. I've had illness and succeeded in getting through it. Having a regular income is a benefit. It doesn't solve everything, but it's a great help.'

Sue Nicholls

AS
AUDREY ROBERTS

When Gail Tilsley's mother, Audrey Potter, arrived in the *Street* in 1979, she gained a reputation as a man-eater. The years have mellowed Audrey – just slightly – and she has become the faithful wife of Alf Roberts, who fights a perennial battle to stop her spending all his hard-earned money.

Actress Sue Nicholls could soon be hearing the sound of wedding bells in real life – if she finds the time. She and actor Mark Eden, who played the *Street*'s Mr Nasty, Alan Bradley, have been together for more than five years. 'We do intend to be married,' she says, 'but we just haven't got round to it. I'd be totally lost without Mark. We make each other laugh, but we do also row and I shout at him for sitting around reading *The Independent* and doing the crossword.

Born in 1943, the Honourable Susan Frances Harmar Nicholls, daughter of former Tory MP Lord Harmar Nicholls, went to a Staffordshire boarding school, where she excelled at languages. 'I then went to Oxford with my parents to look at various colleges,' she recalls, 'but somewhere along the line I wrote to RADA. I had already written at the age of 15 and was turned down at an audition. My father says I was too young, but I think he's a little too generous. I think it was because I was so bloody awful! Anyway, I auditioned again a couple of years later and was there for two years.'

Then Sue went into repertory theatre. 'I played the maid in *Man In Grey*,' she recalls. 'My parents and paternal grandparents were up in the circle and Grandfather Nicholls, who was bad-sighted, was heard to say rather loudly, "Has Sue been on yet?" Most of the people in the circle heard it!'

Television fame came when Sue took the part of Marilyn Gates in *Crossroads*. During one scene in a nightclub, Marilyn was called on to stand in for a singer who had not arrived. She sang *Where Will You Be*, composed by Tony Hatch, who wrote the *Crossroads* theme music. Sue was then asked to record the song and it was a Top 20 hit, which made her decide to leave the serial and try to make it as a pop star. She released a follow-up single, *All the Way To Heaven* – which, she says, 'sold about two copies'.

After a year of cabaret, Sue returned to the theatre and her work included a summer season with Bob Monkhouse in Bournemouth. Many TV appearances followed, in series such as *The Professionals*, *Up the Elephant and Round the Castle* and *The Fall and Rise of Reginald Perrin*, in which she played Perrin's raunchy secretary.

After appearing in *Coronation Street* on and off for six years, she became a regular in 1985. 'Audrey's not quite so loud and brazen now,' says Sue, 'I've tried to take her down a bit, which fitted in with the fact that she married Alf, who is quite serious and sombre. Likewise, she's brought him up a bit. Some people see in my character things that I don't. I'm stopped all the time by people who say, "Isn't she awful to Alf?" or "Isn't she a cow?" I don't see any of that. He needs to be pushed – that's all.'

William Tarmey AND Liz Dawn

AS JACK AND VERA DUCKWORTH

'Tarmey and Dawn' is the name on the label of a pop single, *I'll Be With You Soon*, recorded by William Tarmey and Elizabeth Dawn in 1989. It has overtones of a music-hall double-act, and that is just what Bill and Liz have become in modern TV terms, following in the footsteps of the dear departed Stan and Hilda Ogden.

It was in 1974 that irrepressible actress Liz Dawn first infiltrated the *Street*. Actually, you couldn't miss her, or at least her character – foghorn-voiced Vera, with a cigarette-inspired cackle that sounded like a roll of thunder. She was one of the denim girls in Mike Baldwin's factory. It was 1983, however, before the battling Duckworths – Vera, Jack and their wayward son Terry – actually took up residence in Coronation Street by securing the keys to No 9, one-time home of the Barlows and the Faircloughs.

Like Stan Ogden, Jack started out as a workshy layabout and part-time jack-of-all-trades, from window-cleaner to taxi driver. He first turned up on screen at Brian and Gail Tilsley's wedding in 1979. With an eye for the ladies, he became the oldest swinger in town, with his open-chested, ruffled silk shirt and his gold-plated medallion. Like Stan in his younger days, he had a 'bit of stuff' a few streets away, Dulcie Froggatt (played by Marji Campi – later to appear in *Brookside*).

'But Jack has settled down and matured a bit,' says Bill. 'He has accepted things with a kind of middle-aged resignation. His "birding" days are over, though he relishes the thought of being near his current greatest loves – booze and barmaids. Jack has a strange kind of moral code. He would never

knowingly hurt people and he loves Vera, even though he doesn't always like her. He will defend her to the death, unless the chap slagging her off is bigger than he is! Jack is not a thief, either. If ever the scriptwriters suggested he should dip his hand into the till, I would protest. Of course, he'll drink Alec Gilroy's beer while he is down in the cellar until the cows come home. He regards that as a perk of the job.'

Behind the Jack and Vera story lies an even more fascinating tale of two actors who have risen from modest beginnings, without any formal drama training in terms of theatre school or rep, to become national heroes in the eyes of millions.

Elizabeth Dawn was put to work in a clothing factory – just like Vera – at fifteen. 'I hated every minute of it,' said Leeds-born Liz, 'and I was determined to get out. I was on the bulb counter at Woolworth's at one stage. Then, I went through a phase where I was doing a day job, working as an usherette in the cinema at night, and singing in working men's clubs at weekends. I cut out the regular stage work years ago, but I occasionally do a spot at a bingo hall or something like that.'

Liz's real name is Sylvia Ibbetson, but husband Don, who was also her manager at one point, gave her a stage name that incorporated their daughter's christian name. They have four grown-up children, Graham, Dawn, Ann-Marie and Julie. Liz insists that getting cast in the *Street* was simply a result of being in the right place at the right time. 'You've a better chance of winning the football pools than getting into *Coronation Street*,' she says.

But she is far too modest. Alan Parker, who directed the feature films *Fame* and *Bugsy Malone*, was among the first to recognise her comic talents when he recruited her for a TV commercial. Liz's career might have taken a different twist altogether. Comedian Larry Grayson wanted to sign her up for a major TV series, but she was already committed to *Coronation Street* by then. In between, she worked her way up the ladder via TV commercials and bit parts. She also appeared in outstanding plays such as the BBC's award-winning *Kisses at Fifty*, was a waitress in Granada TV's popular spoof on Northern club life, *The Wheeltappers' and Shunters' Social Club*, and appeared in *The Greenhill Pals*, Granada's moving play about World War One veterans.

Gravel-voiced Bill Tarmey's rise to fame has been just as long and hard. He grew up in the ordinary, working-class Bradford district of Manchester and did a variety of jobs early on, from working in the building trade to running a shop. Unlike 'bird-hunting' Jack, Bill met and married his childhood sweetheart. They celebrated their Silver Wedding in 1977 and have two grown-up children, Carl and Sara.

For 22 years, Bill made a solid living as a singer on the club and cabaret circuit, working with show bands. His real name is William Cleworth Piddington. 'I went to sing at a charity "do" at the Tramways Club in Stockport,' says Bill. 'I asked the concert secretary why my name wasn't up in lights outside the club with the rest. "It is," he said, and pointed to the name Bill Tarmey. "I couldn't fit Piddington in," he said, "and I thought you sounded like Mel Torme, so I changed it to Tarmey." And I have stuck with it ever since.'

It was his singing, initially, that led him towards TV 'extra' work and it just built and built, until he joined the *Street* on a

▼ *Jack and Vera Duckworth are often at each other's throats, but William Tarmey and Elizabeth Dawn have never had a cross word*

regular basis.

Millions of Street fans were alarmed and upset in 1987 when Bill had a relapse after undergoing major heart surgery. 'I was a mess,' reveals Bill. 'At one stage, I ballooned up to over fifteen stone and was smoking fifty cigarettes a day. I couldn't walk a hundred yards without fighting for breath. It was open-heart surgery or curtains. I was out of the show for eighteen weeks – Jack was down the cellar for an awful long time! Now, I'm running around again like a startled fawn.' A slimline Bill weighs in at thirteen-and-a-half stone. 'I have been down to twelve stone, but I look as if I've just climbed out of the ground – it doesn't suit me,' says Bill. Wife Alma has him permanently on a high fibre diet. 'I love food and I would eat all day if she'd let me,' admits Bill.

Tarmey and Dawn are two of the funniest people on TV and Bill insists that, since they got together professionally in 1979, they have never had a cross word. 'Liz is delightfully zany,' he says, 'but she is a real soft touch, especially when it comes to charity. She sometimes gets into terrible fixes by over-committing herself, and then it's panic stations.'

It was Liz, noticing that deaf people were missing out on the fun at public appearances, who determined to learn sign-language. Meanwhile, Bill gives thanks of a different kind by energetically supporting the British Heart Foundation as a gesture towards the local Manchester hospital that saved his life.

Thelma Barlow AND Peter Baldwin

AS MAVIS AND DEREK WILTON

More than 30 years ago, when Thelma Barlow and Peter Baldwin were working together in their first repertory theatre job, they had no idea that they would later form a double-act in television's top programme. Based in Exmouth, Devon, the touring company did one-night performances all over the West Country, travelling in a battered van and erecting the sets at a different theatre each day, sometimes with journeys of more than a hundred miles between venues. 'It was tremendously hard work,' recalls Thelma, 'but they were wonderful days. What it was to be young and energetic!' Later, at Bristol's Old Vic theatre, they starred in *The Way of the World*, playing the husband and wife who were never actually seen together on stage.

Thelma spent most of her career on the stage and appeared in many classical productions, before breaking into television, in plays and serials such as *Vanity Fair*. She joined *Coronation Street* in 1972 as Mavis Riley, a former schoolfriend of Emily Nugent. At Emily's wedding to Ernest Bishop, Mavis met Jerry Booth, but their friendship finished when he revealed that he was divorced. She worked as a vet's receptionist and at the corner shop before Rita Fairclough employed her in the Kabin.

After many years of living alone with budgie Harriet, Mavis found Derek Wilton and Victor Pendlebury fighting for her affections. When Derek won and they were set for the altar, the couple jilted each other – neither turned up at the church for the wedding. It took them a few years to get back together and go through with the marriage. Now, apart from a failed attempt by Victor to rekindle the flames of his relationship with

Mavis, the couple are firmly together and living in Coronation Street itself, after starting married life in the flat above the Kabin.

Thelma puts the *Street*'s success down to its richness of characters. 'It's a special way of playing the parts,' she says. 'It isn't like anything else I've come across. It's heightened realism. Sometimes, very good actors have come in and it hasn't worked for them. They think you just have to be realistic, but you have to take realism and give it a nudge. All the characters are very different from one another – it's a wonderful mish-mash. Then, the storyline writers and scriptwriters and the production side make sure the programme is a very good mix of comedy and serious drama.'

Thelma was born in Middlesbrough five weeks after her father died of pneumonia. She worked as a secretary for seven years, before joining Joan Littlewood's Theatre Workshop in East London. Now divorced with two grown-up sons, she enjoys weekends at her North Yorkshire cottage, where she has an organic garden. 'I became aware that it was so easy to go into a garden centre and buy poisonous things,' she says. 'I don't want to eat that. Nor do I want to spoil the genuine balance of nature. Son Clive, who has a degree in agricultural economics, now manages an off-licence and younger son James, who has a philosophy degree, has become a theatre director, working mostly on fringe productions.

Peter Baldwin has his own brand of theatre directing. He collects nineteenth-century toy theatres and sells them at his London shop, Pollock's, in Covent Garden. 'For years, I was connected with Pollock's Toy Museum and worked there when I wasn't acting,' he says. 'They started a shop in 1980 and asked me if I would manage it for them, so I said I would part-manage it. Eventually, the woman who owned Pollock's decided that having the shop as well as the museum was too much of a responsibility when her husband died. I agreed to take it over, without really thinking it through. Then, my wife went into hospital, where she died, and I couldn't even think about the shop. My brother asked if I'd like him to come in with me. He resigned his job and we took it over. It's purely a toy shop. We concentrate on traditional toys – anything but plastic – and model theatres. It's something quite different from acting, although you're performing there all the time because some people come knowing that I'm in the *Street*. Others are quite surprised.'

It was when Peter was returning to his role as Derek just before Christmas 1987 that his actress wife, former *Play School* presenter Sara Long, died suddenly of cancer. He carried on in true showbusiness fashion to avoid upsetting the *Street* storyline. 'I didn't know quite what to do.' recalls Peter. 'The consultant said it was better for me to keep working. Then, I had a call to say Sara was having a second operation and could I go down to London. I was there for several days. Until the last day, you don't believe it's happening, although I think I knew she was going to die. Going back to work in the *Street* was a good thing for me. It meant I had something I could immediately concentrate on. Then, I told my agent I didn't want to leave London for at least six months. Shortly after that, I was offered a contract as a regular in the *Street*.'

One problem that sometimes afflicts Peter is his sense of humour. 'I'm a great giggler,' he says, 'and find it very difficult to stop laughing. If I'm with a group of people all with sparkling eyes, it gets worse. Once, an aunt of Mavis's died and, after the cremation, there was a funeral tea, involving me, Thelma, Bryan Mosley, Eileen Derbyshire and Barbara Knox. We were sitting around in a little group, talking about cremations. It's not a funny subject, but it is. Finally, Bryan had to say, "Did she want to be cremated?" and we fell about laughing. It got worse and worse in rehearsals and, when we got into the studio to record, we just couldn't speak. Eventually, we were sent home and had to come in early the following morning to do it.'

Lynne Perrie

Ivy Brennan

Diminutive Lynne Perrie, who has played Ivy since 1979, has her own ideas about being written out of the programme if ever she were to leave. She would love Ivy to 'die with her boots on' as an OAP in the Rovers Return. 'Put it this way,' says Lynne, 'if I ever leave the *Street*, I will retire. I don't want to do anything else at this stage in my career.'

Born in Rotherham, Yorkshire, Lynne remembers her first cabaret engagement in the Fifties very clearly. 'My husband's uncle told me that the cabaret turn booked for his club had let them down,' recalls Lynne. 'I earned £4.50 that night, at a time when I was only earning £5 for a whole week's work at a stocking factory. That decided me, so I gave up my job and joined the cabaret circuit.'

Lynne's engagements took her to France, Germany, South Africa and America, working with artists such as Sacha Distel and, for twelve concerts, The Beatles. As well as the tough, demanding environment of clubs and cabaret she appeared in TV dramas such as *Slattery's Mounted Foot*, *Leeds United* and *Queenie's Castle*, and had a starring role in the film *Kes*, before she won her spurs in Weatherfield.

It was in 1979 that she was given a regular part in the *Street*. Peter Dudley and Chris Quinten played husband Bert and son Brian.

'Peter had enormous style,' recalls Lynne. 'He was a champagne and top hotels kind of person in private. He also had a wicked sense of humour. Many a time when I was preparing to put one of Ivy's grumpy "faces" on, he would turn to Chris Quinten just before we went on camera and say, "Just look at your mother's face, son – Hitler in knickers!" Then we couldn't act for laughing. I missed Peter terribly after he died in 1984 after two heart attacks.' She also misses Chris Quinten, who left the *Street* in 1989. 'We were just like mother and son,' says Lynne. 'He used to send me flowers on Mother's Day. He used to say that if he hadn't got a real mum he would choose me.'

There was real-life drama for Lynne, too, twelve years ago, when a routine cervical smear test revealed cancer and she underwent a major operation. She went into hospital a second time, for an operation for a faulty heart valve. 'This last two years or so, I have tried to slow things down a bit,' she says. 'Ivy was taking over and it didn't leave me with much time for my personal life.'

After the death of Bert, Ivy's big moment came in June 1988, when she married her second husband, mini-cab driver Don Brennan, played by Geoff Hinsliff. At one point, the scriptwriters were going to make it a modest, register office wedding, but Lynne stepped in. 'Ivy is always going on about her religious beliefs and, being a Catholic myself, I thought it absolutely must be a church wedding,' she says. 'The other factor was that Derrick and I had to get married in Rotherham register office in a hurry because he was about to be called up for National Service and possibly sent overseas. So this was the wedding I never had, in a way. I know the tears I cried during the recording were real enough.'

Away from the studio, Lynne and husband Derrick are animal lovers. 'We have kept greyhounds on and off for fifteen years,' says Lynne, 'so, when one came into the storyline in June 1989, it was great fun.'

Geoff Hinsliff

AS
DON BRENNAN

Geoff Hinsliff's first appearance in *Coronation Street* was in 1963, when he turned up at Jerry Booth's wedding to Myra Dickinson, to be best man. But Dennis Tanner was also expecting that honour. 'I did the *Street* then, when I was 26,' says Geoff, 'and I was very worried about staying in a serial and being typecast. Then I returned about ten years later as a villian. I arranged to meet Bet Lynch for a date to get her out of her flat and burgle it. I still felt then that I would be dead if I stayed in the programme. It used to be that TV producers wouldn't cast you in anything else because 20 million people knew you in a particular role. Now, it's more that they *want* to cast you because of that. So, when I was offered a contract to play Don Brennan, I was fifty and thought, "What does it matter now?" If you are young and have a whole career ahead of you, *Coronation Street* can be alarming in that it can come to a full stop. At the age of 50, your career is coming to a close or, at least, you have a body of work behind you and people know you can do different things.'

Leeds-born Geoff studied at RADA after doing National Service and played mostly classical roles on stage during his early career. He has performed at London's Old Vic and Royal Court theatres, as well as in the West End. He was in the films *A Bridge Too Far* and *O Lucky Man!* and his many TV appearances include *Z-Cars*, *Softly, Softly*, *Striker*, *Accident* and the original series of *Brass*, in which he played George Fairchild.

Bill Podmore, who in 1987 was *Coronation Street*'s producer and had made *Brass*, invited Geoff to join the serial as Don Brennan. 'Within four months, Don was married to Ivy Tilsley, which was a bit of a shock to

us,' says Geoff. 'Lynne Perrie and I both thought we would have a nice, long courtship first. Suddenly, we got the script and we were getting married.' Don is a loyal husband to Ivy, but he does have a rough side to him and a weakness for gambling. 'He's just a mini-cab driver,' says Geoff, 'and mini-cab drivers tend to be on the shady side of the law. They squabble with real taxi drivers and live on their wits a bit. Don does all these dodgy things, gambling and getting into trouble. Ivy has to worry like hell about him. Don's also had trouble with Mike Baldwin over Ivy, but that's absolutely justifiable. He comes out with his socialist principles when he tackles Baldwin about the way he works and makes money, but he's right. Sweatshops really do still exist. Women who work at home really are very poorly paid and, of all the industries, the rag trade still has sweated labour in that sense. Then, Don was in court for hitting a lad who stole his cab. There's always a reason for the trouble he gets into. I sympathise with Don's hot-headedness. I'm a volatile person myself but, like Don, I never hold personal grudges and I play *him* like that. As a boy in Leeds, there were five of us in our family and we were real Yorkshire and dogmatic, and called a spade a spade, so you had to shout loud to be heard.'

At weekends, Geoff returns to wife Judith and teenage daughters Gabrielle and Sophie at their Essex home. 'I quite like gardening, but I don't get much chance to do it,' he says. 'I drive all the way home, then get out of the car and drive the lawn mower. By then, it's time to go back to Manchester! I have been keeping bees, but I'll have to give it up. I don't need a pile of things to do when I get home.'

Barbara Knox

AS

RITA FAIRCLOUGH

When Rita Fairclough's lover Alan Bradley tried to kill her, the TV audience ratings soared even beyond *Coronation Street*'s own records. Almost 27 million viewers tuned in to some of the serial's most dramatic scenes, in an episode that was the most watched TV programme of the Eighties. Actress Barbara Knox, who plays gutsy Rita, is still astonished at the impact of the story, which evolved over 18 months. 'It was a highlight of my life in the *Street* to have such a wonderful story and for it to last for so long and be so exciting,' she says.

Widowed Rita had fallen for Alan Bradley, father of her foster-daughter Jenny, but she was to be heartbroken when he left her for another woman. Overjoyed at his return, she eventually found out that he was defrauding her by using the deeds on her house to finance his burglar-alarm business. When she confronted him, he attempted to murder her but was interrupted in the nick of time by Jenny's panic-stricken return from her 18th birthday party. After going on the run, Alan was caught by police and held on remand, only to be set free when his case came to court, on the grounds that he had been in jail long enough – after police changed a charge of attempted murder to one of assault. When Rita had a nervous breakdown and disappeared, *Street* residents feared that Alan had killed her, but Bet and Alec Gilroy found her in Blackpool. Alan followed, chased Rita across a street and was hit by a tram, killing him instantly.

Viewer response to the Rita–Alan saga was remarkable. Barbara received thousands of letters, first warning her of what Alan was doing behind Rita's back, then telling their own similar tales. 'People said they had cried with me,' says Barbara. 'They advised Rita to get rid of Alan. Women who had been through the same thing themselves wrote, as did some couples who had done so and come out of it still together, which I find remarkable. One letter was written at two in the morning. The couple had sat, holding hands, watching a scene where Rita went to Alan to ask him to come back to her and didn't know what he had plotted. They said it was very disturbing to see something done so realistically, that they had been through that and had been terrible to each other, but they had got through it, thank God. It took months to answer all the letters I received, but I replied to every one of them because people write to you as a friend.'

Barbara's sustained performances as she acted out Rita's agonies were honoured with the *TV Times* 1989 Best Actress on TV award. It came after years of working in all parts of the showbusiness world. Born in Oldham, the daughter of a foundry worker, Barbara Mullaney left school at 15 to work as a Post Office telegraphist, then in offices, shops and factories. She fulfilled her schoolgirl dream to go on stage when, after some amateur performances, she was invited to join Oldham Rep, one of the many *Street* cast members to learn the business there. She appeared on TV in *Emergency – Ward 10*, *Mrs Thursday*, *Never Mind the Quality, Feel* the Width, The Dustbinmen and A Family at War, performed in many radio plays and had a small role in the film Goodbye, Mr Chips.

In 1969, Barbara had a serious operation and nearly died, so she gave up showbusiness and decided to concentrate on being a wife and mother. She and first husband Denis, a sales manager, had a daughter, Maxine. But, three years later, she was offered the role of Rita Littlewood in Coronation Street, with no suggestion that the character would become a regular member of the cast. At first, Rita lived with construction worker Harry Bates, acting as his wife and the mother of his two children, but she was later to marry Len Fairclough. The couple built up the Kabin newsagent's business together and, for a short time, fostered troubled teenager Sharon Gaskell – played by actress Tracie Bennett, seen more recently in the BBC's Making Out – who caused a sensation when she tried to seduce married Brian Tilsley. Then, after six years of marriage, Len died in a motorway accident in 1983. Rita's heartbreak was compounded by the realisation that the motorway journey led to Bolton and another woman.

During her first few years in the Street, Barbara accepted offers of other work as both actress and singer. At the end of 1975, she collapsed through overwork and took a break from the serial. But she had already achieved an early ambition – to make a record. Her Street character was often seen as a nightclub singer and, when she sang The Party's Over during a concert at the Rovers Return, a record executive heard her and offered a recording contract. The result was an LP called On the Street Where I Live, released in 1973.

Barbara Mullaney, as she still was then, took second husband John Knox's surname when they married in the late 1970s, after her divorce. Barbara prefers to keep her home and screen lives totally separate. 'It's very necessary to keep my private life private,' she says. 'If you are in a programme with such a high profile, it's a very demanding mistress. I try very hard to have a life away from the studios.'

She has one ambition left. 'I would love to do a superb TV commercial like the Martini ads with Leonard Rossiter and Joan Collins,' she says. 'It would be wonderful to leave behind just one superb commercial that's funny and sophisticated.'

▲ Running the Kabin has been one constant thread in Rita Fairclough's troubled life

Bill Waddington

S noopers, busybodies, nosy parkers . . . every street has one, and none more so than in soap operas, where they are very popular with viewers. 'Actually, Percy only became nosy parker-in-chief after Hilda Ogden left in 1987,' says Bill Waddington. 'Before that, she was the one with an ear for everybody's business.'

The philosophy of snooping is something that Bill has researched. 'I have discovered that you are only a busybody when you are older,' he says. 'If you are a youngster, you are classed as merely inquisitive. I agree to a point. If you are not inquisitive as a child, then you learn nowt. In Percy's defence, everything he says and does is well-meant. He is very sincere. I've had letters from people asking me to look into a particular cause because Percy gets things done. One old lady wrote to me and asked, "Can you arrange cheaper phone calls for pensioners because our MP is useless." '

In real life, however, Bill Waddington – or 'Waddy', as he is affectionately known to cast members – enjoys the good life, drives an up-to-the-minute, high-powered saloon car, and owns a string of racehorses. His career stretches back to the heyday of variety and music-hall, when he topped the bill as a well paid comic and toured with the greats, from Sophie Tucker to Lena Horne.

Bill was born in Oldham, Lancashire, in 1916, the son of publicans. He learned to play the ukelele and it came in handy in World War Two when he was recruited for an army concert party called The Blue Pencils.

After the war, at a time when Britain was hungry for entertainment, he became a full-time entertainer and in 1950, in his proudest moment, he performed in a Royal Variety Show before the present Queen Mother.

After bit-parts in TV series such as *A Family at War*, he appeared with Victoria Wood, Julie Walters and Nat Jackley in the 1979 award-winning play *Talent*.

Joining *Coronation Street* in the Eighties was like coming home for Bill. His old mates from music-hall – Betty Driver, Tom Mennard, Len Marten and Jill Summers – were also in the programme. Sadly, Tom has since died, but the *Street* has become so much a part of Bill's life that he has asked Granada Television to keep him under contract until he dies in harness. 'I make no concessions to age,' he says. 'You are as old as you feel. Percy is only a youngster of 68, and I don't feel any different.'

Despite his amazing early broadcasting career, in which he reckons he clocked up more than 800 programmes, mainly in radio shows, Bill regards his role in *Coronation Street* as his finest triumph. 'I have two lovely daughters, Denise and Barbara,' he says, 'but my great sadness is that my late wife Lillian, with whom I had thirty-two wonderful years of wedded bliss, is not here to see me in my finest hour. She died of cancer in 1982.'

Despite his hectic television schedule, Bill is a tireless worker for charity. The elderly and animals are two of his dearest causes. 'I work hard all week,' says Bill, 'so on Sunday mornings I often slip off to stables in Leicestershire, Shropshire and Staffordshire, where my horses are based. I go armed with packets of Polo mints, which they love. We all have a special day out.'

Jill Summers

AS

PHYLLIS PEARCE

Remarkable as it might seem, Jill Summers is 80 the day after *Coronation Street* celebrates its 30th anniversary – and she has been in showbusiness all her life. With a circus tightrope walker father and a revue artist mother, she found herself on the stage at an early age and went on to become a stand-up comedienne for many years. 'I've played every theatre in London and every theatre in the provinces,' she says. 'Most of them have gone now, but I've had the best of everything – theatre and television.'

Her TV appearances have included the series *This Year, Next Year, Castle Haven* – which included the *Street*'s Roy Barraclough in its cast – and her own show, *Summers Here*, featuring guests such as comedian Michael Bentine and *Bergerac* actor Terence Alexander.

Jill's happiest memory was appearing with the *Street* cast in the 1989 Royal Variety Performance and meeting the Queen afterwards. They had met twice before when her doctor husband, now dead, was honoured by Her Majesty. 'When my husband died, six years ago, the *Coronation Street* cast saved my reason,' she recalls. 'They made me live again.'

Her first appearance in the serial was as Hilda Ogden's fellow-cleaner at a nightclub, but she later returned as Phyllis Pearce, of the blue-rinse hairdo. Man-mad Phyllis was furious at losing her job in Jim's Café but now

spends all her hours chasing Percy Sugden. 'Percy can't stand Phyllis,' says Jill, 'but he does use her. Wherever he goes, she chases him. There really are boring men like him that women think are marvellous. He can do no wrong for Phyllis, talking about Burma and the war. She's very lonely, really, and all she can think of is Percy, even though she knows he doesn't want her, but he's her life.'

Jill, who has an adopted son and two grandchildren, lives in Yorkshire and enjoys reading her fan-mail. 'I have lots of letters from kids,' she says. 'They think I'm ever so funny and say I should be their grandmother. Wherever I go, the kids recognise me immediately – they come up to me and say they love the character I play. They always call me Phyllis, of course. Even when people can't see me I get recognised – my voice is a giveaway. When my fence came down in the storms, I phoned for a handyman, and his wife answered. When he came round, he said, "It *is* you. My wife said she was sure from the voice it was Phyllis from *Coronation Street.*"'

Helen Worth

A S

GAIL TILSLEY

Helen Worth is one of *Coronation Street*'s more reticent stars. Her character, Gail Tilsley, has been through marriage, divorce, remarriage, motherhood and widowhood, but Helen prefers to keep her own private life well under wraps, apart from confirming that, yes, she does live with *Boys From the Blackstuff* actor Michael Angelis. 'I love my cottage in Cheshire and I have a flat in London,' she says. 'It's a hectic schedule working on the *Street*, but Mike and I try to be together as much as we can. Time has been taken off all the cast since going to three episodes a week. I started learning French, but there's no time now.' Helen declines to say whether she and Michael have plans to marry but, approaching 40, she has no regrets about not having had children. 'Not at all,' she adds.

The elfin-faced actress was born in Leeds but grew up in Morecambe, Lancashire. Her grandmother ran a theatrical boarding-house in Bradford, where music-hall stars stayed. Helen began dancing lessons at the age of three to correct a tendency to walk with her toes turning inwards. Soon, she wanted to go on the stage. She had her first television role at the age of 10 in an episode of *Z-Cars* that also included Glenda Jackson. 'I saw that on a TV quiz programme recently,' says Helen, 'and the contestants recognised me but not Glenda!' Two years later, her parents took her to London for a twelfth birthday treat and allowed her to audition to play one of the children in the West End production of *The Sound of Music*. She was offered the role, which meant staying with a chaperone in London for nine months, before returning home to Morecambe and finishing her schooling.

At 15, Helen went to a stage school in London for a year, then went into repertory theatre. 'That's where I learned my trade,' she says. 'I started in Northampton and played an enormous variety of roles there, which is how you learn to do it.' She worked in theatres in Hornchurch, Watford and Richmond-upon-Thames, and then did BBC radio repertory work for a year, playing anything from a two-year-old to a grandmother, but usually roles younger than her own age. There was also television work, including *Doctor Who*, before she landed the role of Gail Potter in *Coronation Street* in 1974. 'It was my third attempt at getting into the *Street*,' she says, 'but I landed a gem with Gail.' The thought of working with Violet Carson, Jack Howarth and the serial's other stars terrified Helen initially, but she soon settled in.

'Gail's had an extraordinary life,' says Helen. 'She came in as a girl and is now a woman, and has been through all the problems we all go through. She's a very earthy character. I think people relate to her and react to her well. Getting together with Martin was a surprise, something I didn't expect, but that's what we're here for. I thought it was a good story and enjoyed doing it. I like Gail a lot. I'm not married and I don't have children, but I could have been like her if I had stayed in Morecambe as a young girl.'

Amanda Barrie

ALMA SEDGEWICK

It always seemed natural that Amanda Barrie should go into showbusiness. She was born in Ashton-under-Lync, Lancashire, where her grandfather owned a theatre, and started dancing and singing there at the age of three. Amanda later trained at a ballet school and, in her early teens, travelled to London to appear in *Babes In the Wood* pantomime at the Finsbury Park Empire.

Since her early days as a chorus girl, she has been in numerous London West End productions. 'The happiest memories have always related first to who one worked with, not what the production was,' says Amanda. 'I desperately enjoyed playing opposite Paul Eddington in *Absurd Person Singular* and *Donkey's Years*. We played husband and wife in both plays. It was also a privilege to play with Julia McKenzie in *Stepping Out*.' Her films include *Carry On Cleo* and *One of Our Dinosaurs is Missing*.

The role of Alma Sedgewick, wife of café owner Jim, was just a two-week job for Amanda in 1981. Elsie Tanner had applied for a job at Jim's Café and Alma turned up and

rejected her. 'I shook,' recalls Amanda. 'I looked at all the *Street* actors as if they were their characters, and Pat Phoenix, who played Elsie, was a big personality. I'm very glad I worked with her, albeit for just a short time. She had glamour and was a larger-than-life person, a one-off.'

Amanda did not return to the *Street* until 1989, when Alma – by then divorced from husband Jim – invited Gail Tilsley to go into partnership with her in the café. She was also to find romance with Mike Baldwin, but he dumped her for young Dawn Prescott, only to be dumped himself. Soon, Alma was back in his arms. 'I quite like her being with Mike Baldwin,' says Amanda. 'I know he isn't a goodie, but they make a good couple. I get stopped by little old ladies in the street saying he's a baddie, but others say they're right for each other.'

In real life, Amanda separated from actor husband Robin Hunter more than ten years ago, but they have never divorced. 'It's something we've never got round to,' she says. 'After the marriage broke down, we remained good friends. I think a lot of people find they let things go on and don't do anything. I don't have any plans to marry again, but I'm never foolish enough to open my mouth and say I won't. I'd be very wary about getting married again. There would have to be someone special.'

When Amanda returns to her London flat at weekends, she tries to find time to look for antiques. 'They're not really antiques,' she says. 'I go in for high-style junk! Nothing I have is worth anything, but it's decorative. I like finding things and restoring them, like a Georgian birdcage I have. It gives them another life. I do a lot of rescue jobs, probably because I feel sorry for things that get a bit damaged.'

Watching horse-racing and having the occasional flutter also appeal to Amanda. 'I'm passionately fond of horses,' she says. 'When I was born, there weren't such things as female jockeys, but I did ride. If I'd been born twenty years later and hadn't gone on the stage, I think I would have become a female apprentice. I'm quite glad now that I didn't!'

Sally Whittaker AND Michael Le Vell

AS SALLY AND KEVIN WEBSTER

As Sally and Kevin Webster prepare for parenthood, Sally Whittaker and Michael Le Vell have different ideas about how their characters should develop. 'I'd like them to be the couple of the 1990s,' says Sally. 'It's really important that Sally and Kevin show that having a baby doesn't stop couples doing other things. I'd like this baby to be involved in everything they do, to show people that children aren't such a burden on your life, as has been made out.'

Michael is not so sure. 'I hope the characters won't change too drastically,' he says. But will Kevin be changing nappies? 'I think Sally will make him do those things,' says Sally Whittaker. 'It's hard to think of him doing it, but I think he can be won round. I'd also like Sally to work. Although she's been working in the corner shop, I think she's quite ambitious and would like to go on to do other things. She saves up money and doesn't go out much or on holiday. She's quite a clever young girl.'

Sally, born in Middleton, near Oldham, Lancashire, trained at the Mountview Theatre School, North London, and began her career with *The Metal Mickey Road Show*. She appeared on TV as a heroin addict in *Juliet Bravo* and in *The Practice* before joining *Coronation Street* as Sally Seddon in 1986.

Michael is sure that his character made the right choice in marrying Sally. 'Without a doubt, she was the right one for Kevin,' he says. 'She was everything that he wasn't – quite boisterous, for instance – but they say opposites attract.'

In real life, Michael is married to actress Janette Beverley, who played dizzy Sharon in the comedy series *Sharon and Elsie* and, more recently, has been in the ITV drama *Children's Ward*, made by Granada TV. 'It's quite handy when she's recording in the studios because we can see more of each other,' says Michael.

Before landing the role of Kevin, Michael had already appeared in the *Street* as Neil Grimshaw, a newspaper delivery boy at the Kabin. He was also on TV in programmes such as *My Son, My Son, The Hard Word* and *One By One*. 'Being in the *Street* has enabled me to play in celebrity soccer teams at Wembley twice, Anfield, Goodison Park and Old Trafford,' says Michael, who supports Manchester United and Oldham Athletic.

Michael's fans have been getting used to his clean-shaven look. 'I asked three times for the moustache to come off,' says Michael. 'Then, when I picked up a script earlier this year, it was written in. I'd had it since the age of 15, when I grew it so that I could get into pubs! Even when I was 18, they wouldn't serve me!'

Sally, who is single and enjoys walking over Hampstead Heath when she returns to her London flat at weekends, finds that the agony-aunt role her character sometimes fulfils occasionally spills over into real life. 'My girl friends phone me and talk about things they can't tell other friends,' she says. 'I think I'm probably a good listener.'

Sally Ann Matthews

AS

JENNY BRADLEY

It was good news for the *Street* when Oldham-born Sally Ann Matthews turned up as paper girl Jenny Bradley in 1986. But it turned out to be bad news when Jenny's mother died and father Alan Bradley arrived and won the affections of Rita Fairclough, before attempting to murder her and then getting himself killed by a Blackpool tram. Jenny, who had started studying for a degree at Manchester Polytechnic, blamed Rita and it was a while before they were reconciled. She has since moved into Rita's house in Coronation Street which she now shares with fellow-student Felicity 'Flic' Khan, played by Rita Wolf.

Since joining the cast as a 15-year-old, Sally Ann has grown up and reflects that she might have carried on her education, like Jenny, but for the *Street*. 'I had a tutor at the studios when I was doing my O-levels,' she says. 'I had been planning to have a year off in the big, wide world, then do A-levels. At one point, I wanted to be a speech therapist or go into public relations. If I didn't carry on acting, I would have to do something where I was meeting people. Jenny is independent and career minded, and supposed to be a woman of the 1990s, but I'm not. I don't agree with women's equality being pushed in the way it is. They make it out that men are the enemy. I want to be treated as a woman.'

Sally Ann's boyfriend is Huddersfield Town footballer Michele Cecere. 'He's Italian and opens doors and does all the gentlemanly things. I like all the old-fashioned things, when men were gentlemen.'

When Michele was transferred from Oldham Athletic to Huddersfield Town, Sally Ann moved to Huddersfield to be near him. 'I've never really been ambitious,' she says. 'I never thought I would get the chance to become an actress and I used to daydream about it, but it happened. I'd like to do films, but it wouldn't be the end of the world if I didn't. Once I get married and have children, that will be the main thing.'

Sean Wilson

AS

MARTIN PLATT

It was third time lucky for Sean Wilson when he auditioned for the role of Martin Platt in *Coronation Street*. He had already been turned down as Terry Duckworth and Kevin Webster. 'I came in for six weeks to help out in the café,' says Sean. 'I don't know if the producers had any bigger ideas at that time. It took me a few years to get into it, but my confidence grew as Martin's grew.'

The young actor had begun his career building sets at Oldham Coliseum while on a Youth Training Scheme, then joined the town's famous Theatre Workshop, appearing in a musical, *The Gas Street Kids*. Sean teamed up with a friend to do a cabaret act around pubs and clubs and then returned to

the Theatre Workshop, playing the son in Brecht's *The Mother*. Television work followed, with the role of a skinhead in *Crown Court* and a bit part in *Travelling Man*. Then came a dream role, starring in a Channel Four film, *Mozart's Unfinished*. 'I'd just been to the Glastonbury rock festival,' Sean recalls, 'and my agent phoned and asked where I'd been. We hadn't spoken for about six months because there hadn't been any work, but he told me to get down to Yorkshire TV. When I arrived, all these guys freaked. Apparently, I'm a dead ringer for Mozart. It was a factual programme, with John Julius Norwich interviewing this guy from Leeds University who had decided to finish off some of Mozart's unfinished work. I heard what he had done and it sounded really good. During the dramatised bit, I had to conduct an orchestra. If they had really been following me, it would have sounded more like Led Zeppelin!'

Sean joined *Coronation Street* in 1985 and, four years later, found his character becoming widowed Gail Tilsley's 'toyboy' lover. 'It was a big surprise at the time,' he says, 'and I was a bit wary about it for a couple of days when we were told what was going to happen, but it turned out OK. Martin's a very morally correct person, the way he looks after Gail's children. I don't think of myself being as moral as him! Also, although he's been in trouble with people in the past, it's always been that he was right but was misunderstood. Usually, I'm just wrong.'

Kevin Kennedy

AS

CURLY WATTS

Norman Watts, known to everyone except his former landlady Emily Bishop as Curly, turned down a university place to become a binman because he needed to earn money. Later, after a broken relationship with factory worker Shirley Armitage and when he had finished his studies, he became assistant manager at a supermarket, where a young assistant, Kimberley Taylor, took a fancy to him, but he was very slow on the uptake.

'He is mad,' says Kevin. 'He's always been odd, but he's never boring because you never know what he is going to do next. Once he started working at the supermarket, I could play him as two characters. At the supermarket, he became efficacious and a clone of Mr Holdsworth, the manager, and began to think he was Michael Douglas, with the sleeked-back hair. Then he would leave and become his Leftist self, in jeans and with the hair up. He loves playing the young

executive and lording it over everybody at the supermarket. I think he is too involved in furthering his career to think about women and he was badly hurt last time, so he is keeping his distance with Kimberley. Even Curly isn't completely dim in that way. I like people who make me laugh, and he brings his own brand of wackiness to different scenes.'

Kevin has been playing Curly since 1982 but still gets the chance to play other roles, such as that of Runnicles in the stage play *No Sex Please, We're British* on tour last year. He also plays the guitar in several groups around Manchester and writes music. He says it is just a hobby, but recording companies have shown an interest.

Unlike Curly, Kevin is married. He and wife Dawn have a young son, Ryan. 'He has had a good, stabilising effect on me,' says Kevin, 'although I still go up to the pub with the lads, but not as much as I used to. It's nice to go home and sit Ryan on my knee and listen to what he's been doing all day and who he has been hitting.'

Nicholas Cochrane AND Simon Gregory
AS
ANDY
AND
STEVE MCDONALD

The McDonald twins have been called Bros lookalikes – but, in real life, the teenaged actors are not even brothers. Nicholas Cochrane is also a year older than Simon Gregory. The two were at the same comprehensive school, near Stockport, when *Coronation Street* spotted them.

Nicholas had actually been in the pro-

gramme once before, as an 'extra' playing football in a street scene. All his acting experience had been on the stage for his school. 'I always fancied acting,' he says. 'I used to watch *Grange Hill* and think, "I can do miles better than that." So I did plays and musicals like *My Fair Lady* at primary school and then, later on, a school performance of the Willy Russell play *Our Day Out*, which we performed at the Forum Theatre, Manchester.'

Nicholas, who left school in the summer of 1990, has an immediate goal of passing his driving test. A more long-term ambition is to appear in films.

Simon Gregory takes his GCSEs in the summer of 1991 and has a tutor to help him with his studies at the TV studios. He appeared in plays at primary school but since then had done no acting until he landed his part in *Coronation Street*. He probably kept too busy outside school. Holidays on his father's sailing boat led to his wanting a bit more action on water, so in 1990 he bought himself a speedboat and began water-skiing lessons. As well as his GCSEs, Simon is taking an exam in motor vehicle technology. 'I'm always messing about with my dad's car, opening up the bonnet and tuning up the engine,' he says.

After his exams, Simon will probably continue acting. 'The job I'd really like is as an RAF technician,' he says, 'but I doubt if I'd get the qualifications for that. I was in the RAF cadets and flew a Chipmunk. My dream is to have a log cabin in the woods and an old plane that I could get flying again.'

WHAT THE EYE DOESN'T SEE . . .

Everything that happens in the *Street* begins with the writers. There are normally about eleven of them working for the programme, together with a story editor, two storyline writers and a programme historian. They meet every third Monday, when producer Mervyn Watson chairs a story conference to plan nine episodes, three weeks' worth of *Coronation Street*, which will be seen about three months later.

Copies of the agenda are distributed. It consists mainly of questions such as, 'What has happened to A since we last saw him? Should B get a job and how does this work out? It is C's birthday, how does she celebrate? D needs a story; let's think about her.'

If a proposed storyline requires the return of an actor not seen for some time, Mervyn Watson will ask his production assistant to check on his availability, which she will do while the conference continues. If the actor is committed elsewhere on the appropriate dates, the idea must be amended.

The discussion moves on to an eventual consensus and Mervyn Watson says, 'That's the first episode. Now Episode Two . . .' With time out for lunch, it might take until 5pm to work through the list, for in any one episode it is customary to have at least three stories running, and the team try to keep a balance of drama and comedy, unless comedy would jar in a highly dramatic episode, such as one involving a funeral.

The programme eats stories and it is vital to generate new and fresh ideas. Viewers often write in with story suggestions, but they are rarely usable, mainly because production has already moved far beyond the point viewers have reached. Charities and pressure groups of all kinds also propose storylines hoping to draw attention to their causes, but they are rarely adopted either, unless they inspire an original and dramatic storyline. Some ideas are gleaned from newspaper stories, others are inspired by programme historian Daran Little, who reminds the team of such dates as birthdays and wedding anniversaries. He keeps records of every incident that has been seen on screen, and also unseen events that have been referred to, such as a character's

▲ *Producer Mervyn Watson chairs a story conference, at which storyline writers and scriptwriters thrash out three weeks' worth of episodes*

schooling or early working life. No other British television production maintains such detailed archives.

After the conference, the storyline writers have two weeks in which to prepare detailed synopses of the nine episodes, presenting them in a scene-by-scene breakdown. On the Monday morning of the third week, the producer commissions writers to write the nine episodes. Usually this means nine writers each writing one script, though there are rare occasions when it is felt that a particular pair of scripts would benefit by having one writer handle both.

The writers receive all of the synopses and study them before attending a commissioning conference three days later, when they discuss the continuity of the story and the establishment of any new characters, as a result of which the storylines might be amended. The writers then go away to start work on their episodes and have about two weeks in which to write them. When they deliver them, they will be read by the story editor, storyline writers and producer during the following week to check for continuity, and the scripts will then be handed over to directors.

There are, at any one time, four directors working on the serial in a four-week cycle.

▼ *For once, the production crew (left) line up in front of the studio cameras and (below) cast and crew prepare to record a scene on the Rovers Return set*

Director A collects his three scripts on the first Monday of his four-week turn-around and begins preparations, while director B is in his second week of preparation, Director C is rehearsing and recording, and Director D is editing and dubbing the programmes he has recorded.

When Director A receives his scripts, he studies them, then enters into a series of meetings: with the designer about new sets; with the location planner about any exterior filming, particularly any away from the permanent *Street* lot; with the casting department about new artists; with his production assistant about the administration for rehearsals and recording, and with the producer about any problems he foresees. A significant part of the director's preparation fortnight will be spent studying the rehearsal scripts and preparing his camera scripts, marking perhaps 400 shots to be taken by three cameras. When he has finished work on them, he hands the scripts over to his production assistant, who types out all his instructions on to her script, after which 43 copies are made and distributed to all the people concerned in the production.

The production week starts on Sunday with the filming of any exterior scenes not on the permanent *Coronation Street* lot. On Monday, scenes on the real outside street set itself are filmed. On Tuesday and Wednesday, the director conducts rehearsals of each scene for the three episodes in a bare rehearsal room, where plastic tape on the floor indicates where furniture will be positioned.

On Wednesday afternoon comes the tech-nical run in the rehearsal room, at which the lighting director notes the movements of the artists so that he can draw up his lighting plan, and the senior cameraman and the sound supervisor warn of any difficulties they foresee. The producer also watches the rehearsals, and gives the cast and crew any notes he makes. The production assistant times the episodes. Each is scheduled to run exactly 24 minutes 35 seconds, to allow for commercials and programme announcements. If episodes are more than a minute under time, it will be necessary to consider lengthening a scene or scenes, or introducing a new one. Overruns will be cut, which is easier. Then everyone breaks and prepares for two days in the studio.

On Wednesday night, the lighting director and his electricians light the studio. The designer sees that the prop men put all the props in their right places.

On Thursday, at 9am, the cameramen move in, and rehearsals and recording start. Each scene is rehearsed until everyone is happy, then recorded on videotape. More often than not, for convenience, scenes will be recorded out of chronological sequence in an order arranged by the director. Work goes on until 6.30pm, and starts again at 9am on Friday.

Early the following week, the director and his production assistant move into the editing suite and have about eight-and-a-half hours in which to edit the programmes, which will be transmitted three weeks later, on Monday, Wednesday and Friday. On the following Monday that director's cycle starts again when he collects his next three scripts.

BEHIND THE WORDS

When *Coronation Street* began, Tony Warren had written only twelve scripts, so a team of scriptwriters had to be put together – and quickly. H. V. 'Harry' Kershaw and John Finch had already been taken on by the end of 1960, before the *Street* was a few weeks old. 'Harry and I used to write the story outline and then toss a coin to decide who wrote what,' recalls John. 'I always reckoned he had a two-headed penny because he always got the best episodes.' Harry went on to produce the programme and John became writer of series such as *A Family at War* and *Sam*.

Then, Granada added to the scriptwriting team one-time Liverpool bus driver Cyril Abraham, who later wrote *The Onedin Line*, Jack Rosenthal, who went on to script *The Lovers* and numerous TV plays, Vince Powell and his partner Harry Driver, who subsequently wrote comedy series such as *Nearest and Dearest*, and former *Guardian* journalist Peter Eckersley, who eventually became Granada's head of drama.

Adele Rose, who joined the *Street* during its early days and is still there, was the programme's first female writer. 'It's a democratic set-up,' she says. 'You may take ideas to story conferences, but you have to win over the assembled company before they are implemented. In the end, it's a team effort.'

For more than a decade, Adele and other stalwarts such as Leslie Duxbury, John Stevenson and Barry Hill have been the programme's creative backbone. 'You get your ideas from trips to the supermarket, conversations in shops – wherever you go, just living your life,' says Adele. 'But you also rely a great deal on that mysterious inner source of creative energy – imagination.'

WARDROBE SECRETS

Hilda Ogden's faded cotton pinny, Ena Sharples's black-and-white straw plant-pot hat, and Albert Tatlock's greasy old suit are some of the best-known 'props' in the history of British television. And though the characters are gone, their costumes are lovingly preserved in a quiet corner of Granada's TV Centre in Manchester known as 'The Cave'.

Jack Howarth would never wear anything on screen apart from that one suit, so threadbare that the weave was coming apart at the seams – and he refused to have it dry-cleaned. Lynne Perrie felt the same about her factory overall when new ones were bought. She refused to part with her original.

Flat hats, worn with distinction in the past by Jack Howarth, are now a trademark of Percy Sugden. Upright Alf Roberts has a different line in hats. 'Alf's main props are a trilby and a white overall,' says actor Bryan Mosley, 'but any hat will do for me.'

These fond attachments are quite fortuitous as the weekly *Coronation Street* costume budget is only about £300. In 1972 it was £15. The wardrobe team shop for bargains, buying the same, off-the-peg outfits that most people buy from high street shops. A good example of economy was the cotton tops bought for Sally Whittaker and Elizabeth Dawn, who play Sally Webster and Vera Duckworth, for just £7 each in 1988.

Most characters have at least three outfits: working clothes, casual gear for the evenings and Sunday best. Lynne Perrie, at less than five feet tall, is a particular problem because she needs size 8 to 10 dresses and size 2½ to 3 shoes. When Ivy Tilsley married Don Brennan in 1988, they had to look all over the North West to find a size 10 dress and eventually discovered the right one in Preston.

◀ *Adele Rose was the* Street's *first female scriptwriter*

▶ *Tiny Lynne Perrie poses problems for the programme's wardrobe department*

THE STREET WHERE THEY LIVE

Weatherfield is just a figment of Tony Warren's imagination, but there is a Castlefield – the area of Manchester where Granada's TV Centre and the outdoor street set are situated.

Now, the 'Street of fame' numbers among the area's top tourist attractions. The *Coronation Street* outdoor lot is part of Granada's seven-and-a-half-acre production centre site. Any site expansion is tricky because of strict regulations that control development in this historic area.

The previous outdoor *Street* set, in continuous use since 1970, had reached the end of its useful life and needed to be larger and more authentic. Because it blocked access to the Grape Street Warehouse redevelopment – a building that now contains rehearsal rooms, dressing rooms and make-up areas for 200 actors – it was demolished in 1982 and rebuilt on a new site on the opposite side of the warehouse, where it stands today.

This time, the street was built life-size, instead of the two-thirds scale of the old set. These improvements have made it more flexible for filming and gives an extra dimension of reality to viewers. Thousands of old bricks and tiles were salvaged from the Manchester area to ensure a genuine look. Walking down the street itself, past the exterior brick façade, it is impossible to tell that the inside is just one long, empty space with an upper walkway for actors to appear at first-floor windows, and that the chimney stacks are of glass-reinforced plastic supported on the roof trusses, so avoiding the need for cross-walls.

Because the set is full-size, the street is longer. Computer modelling by Building De-sign Partnership, architects to this skilful piece of TV redevelopment, assessed the effect of this upgrading on camera angles and gauged the visual impact of adjacent buildings.

At one point, visitors were able to stroll down Coronation Street, then, in a couple of strides, turn the clock back to the era of Hansom cabs and gas lamps by walking straight into Baker Street, Granada's outdoor lot for the TV adventures of Sherlock Holmes, starring Jeremy Brett.

Now, *Coronation Street* visitors from all over the world, who used to be reduced to peering over high walls before the Granada Studios Tour was opened, can also spend an intriguing hour or two browsing round the nearby Air and Space Museum and the Manchester Museum of Science and Technology, which is stuffed with fascinating working engines and relics salvaged from the Industrial Revolution.

The tour, which started in July 1988, covers a three-and-a-half-acre site. Visitors can stroll past Alf Roberts's Mini Market to the Rovers Return, along the most famous cobbled street in the world, examine the houses from every angle – including the backyards, browse through the wardrobe department, where Bet Gilroy's wedding dress and Ena Sharples's best hat and coat are kept, pose for a picture in the Rovers' Snug, look around the *Coronation Street* Museum, and buy memorabilia, such as replicas of Hilda Ogden's flying ducks. Via Chromakey, a system that superimposes one television image over another, you can even appear in a *Street* scene and buy the video to treasure for ever. Other attractions on the tour include sets from major Granada TV series such as *Game, Set & Match* and *First Among Equals*. Visitors are also shown the techniques of programme direction and make-up. In its first year, 600,000 people went on the Granada Studios Tour and it won two major tourism awards, from the English Tourist Board and the British Tourist Authority. Visitors are advised to book in advance (telephone 061-833 0880) because sometimes the 'House Full' signs have to be put up.

WHAT THE PAPERS SAID
ABOUT MIKE, KEN AND DEIRDRE

▲ *The action hots up as Deirdre Barlow falls for* Street *romeo Mike Baldwin*

Newspapers' obsession with soap operas, and *Coronation Street* in particular, has never been more clearly illustrated than when, in 1983, a domestic fracas in the Barlow household generated a bout of media hysteria of the kind normally reserved for high society scandals and the daily affairs of royalty. The Ken–Mike–Deirdre affair was described as the most volatile and explosive storyline in the programme's history to that point.

Deirdre had all the things that a young housewife yearns for – a nice daughter, a comfortable home, a good husband. Everything except a little excitement and romance in her life. When smoothtalker Baldwin came

along, Deirdre – hardly your typical adultress – fell for his cockney charms at a Community Centre Cabaret Night. Within four weeks, all hell had broken loose and the popular press were laying siege to Granada's Manchester TV Centre.

The innocuous storyline issued by Granada for the episode of Wednesday 19 January 1983 read, 'Mike Baldwin takes Deirdre Barlow to a posh restaurant on a secret dinner date. "Don't worry" he tells her, "you're not going to meet anybody from round Coronation Street in here. You're not nervous are you?" "A bit," says Deirdre, because she had told her husband Ken that she was going to see her friend Carol.' Ken

Tossell, of the *Daily Mirror*, described the event as 'the most explosive, romantic situation in the history of *Coronation Street*.'

As the great cliffhanger unfolded, there was wide media conjecture over whether Deirdre should go to bed with Mike, or even leave Ken to go and live with him. Yet the programme itself, as befits a family saga, was a model of propriety. The final screen climax was, in fact, no more than a modest kiss. Nevertheless, the *Sunday Mirror* decided to consult a marriage guidance councillor in a story headlined 'Don't Be Too Hasty Deirdre'.

The *Daily Star* asked the viewer in the street how Deirdre should resolve her dilemma? 'To a man,' said the *Star*, 'they believe that Deirdre should go ahead and have her fling.' The *Daily Mail* then assigned its problem page and women page editors to assess the situation. 'No, no, no, Deirdre – don't do it,' wrote one. 'Go on Deirdre – get stuck in!' wrote the other.

On Sunday 30 January, a London bishop writing in the *Sunday Mirror* warned the Granada production team, 'Don't be too realistic – it might backfire.' As the suspense began to generate record viewing figures, Fleet Street wheeled its big guns into action. The *Daily Mail*'s Lynda Lee Potter said that Deirdre should go ahead because an affair would rejuvenate her tired marriage to boring Ken! Rival columnist Jean Rook, writing in the *Daily Express* said, 'Don't wander off into the mire with Mike, Deirdre – stick in the mud with Ken!'

The *Sun* asked a computer if Mike and Deirdre were compatible, while Tyne Tees Television faced a barrage of complaints from North East viewers. There had been a breakdown in transmission and the fans demanded an action-replay of the 'kissing' episode.

As media interest continued to boil over, *The Times* felt obliged to run a 'story so far' for its up-market readers. A Halifax housewife was reported to have had her baby in the ambulance on the way to hospital – delayed because she wanted to see Mike and Deirdre in a clinch. The *Sunday Mirror*, not wanting to lose ground on its rivals, roared from its front page, 'Is Deirdre Pregnant?' The basis for this flimsy piece of speculation turned out to be a joke circulating in the Granada office pub. Poet Laureate Sir John

Betjeman, a devoted *Street* fan, made his preference known by proclaiming, 'I think Ken is a nice man and he deserves better.'

Desperate for a new angle in what had now become the Mike–Ken–Deirdre circulation war, the *Daily Star* forecast a baby boom in nine months' time because, it said, 'women are staying away from family planning clinics in favour of watching *Coronation Street*'. Next the *Daily Telegraph* solemnly reported that MP Cyril Smith's brother Norman had tried to adjourn a Rochdale Council committee early 'so that we can all watch Ken and Deirdre'. Stanley Reynolds, TV critic of the *Manchester Evening News*, compared the *Street* with Ibsen and pronounced, 'I rather think Ibsen comes off second best.' The *Guardian* reported that a Chesterfield theatre had sold only one ticket for a performance 'the night Ken and Deirdre were on the telly'.

Keith Waterhouse, writing dryly in his *Daily Mirror* column, propounded, 'When the nation is deeply divided over an important issue, should taxpayers' money be spent on backing one side against the other? . . . The government favours a zero option for Mike and Deirdre, with the retention of Uncle Albert as the ultimate deterrent.'

The *Sun* claimed that the Queen had phoned Buckingham Palace from Mexico with strict instructions that that night's episode of *Coronation Street* must be taped and flown out to her in South America.

For sheer enterprise, the *Daily Mail* takes the biscuit. Realising there would be a captive audience of 56,000 fans at Old Trafford for the Manchester United versus Arsenal soccer match, they hired the electronic scoreboard to flash a message on the night of the crucial *Street* episode in which Ken threatened to evict Deirdre from their home, because transmission clashed with the kick-off time. During the match the scoreboard flashed up the message, 'Deirdre and Ken united again. Read tomorrow's *Daily Mail* for an action-replay of tonight's match and the *Coronation Street* re-match.' The Stretford Enders cheered like mad.

The story that gripped the nation ultimately earned its stars just recognition for their performance. Anne Kirkbride, William Roache and Johnny Briggs were named TV Personalities of the Year in the 1983 Pye Colour Television Awards.

. . . AND WHAT THEY SAID ABOUT KEN, DEIRDRE AND WENDY

Ken had held on to wife Deirdre but when he was to fall into another woman's arms almost seven years later she would not fight for him in the same way. As his affair with council secretary Wendy Crozier – played by Roberta Kerr – developed after she leaked confidential information to his local newspaper, the real journalists in London and all over the country were slow to realise that this was to become another explosive drama in the Barlow household.

On 21 December 1989, Jaci Stephen wrote in the London *Evening Standard*, 'Drama surrounding The Other Woman or The Other Man is always popular among viewers, and I suspect that the Christmas Day edition of *Coronation Street* will prove the most popular seasonal programme of all time.' Certainly, the episode topped the 1989 Christmas TV ratings, but not before William Roache told the *Daily Mirror* on 23 December, 'I don't envy Ken. He's about to find out the price he will have to pay for having an affair . . . You can't have a grimmer Christmas than trying to pretend to a child while she opens her presents that everything is all right when it clearly could not be any worse.'

Some newspapers thought the Barlow's Christmas was not grim enough. Ken had admitted his affair to Deirdre in the preceding episode and TV critics had been hoping for all hell to be let loose. Under the headline 'Dead-End Street', on 26 December, Hilary Kingsley wrote in the *Daily Mirror*, 'No flying plates, no floods of tears. The black looks were only mid-grey. If that was The Big Showdown between Ken and Dreary over his adultery with Wendy built-like-a-bull-terrier Crozier I can only say I've had better rows with my goldfish.'

The Scottish *Sunday Mail* reflected the general anti-Ken feeling. Dorothy Johnson wrote, 'Trust old misery-guts Ken Barlow to be the Christmas party-pooper. The flabby Casanova of *Coronation Street* spent the week looking as though someone had shoved a sprig of holly down his thermals!

Looking back, on the last day of the year, the *People* wrote that *Coronation Street* had won the battle of the soaps in 1989 with the most nail-biting stories in its 29-year-history, and 'Deirdre Barlow's tearful discovery of husband Ken's fling' was one of four major stories it highlighted. As Ken was under pressure to choose between his wife and mistress, the *Daily Star* laid before its readers the story purportedly as seen through the eyes of Ken, Deirdre, daughter Tracy and lover Wendy, and invited readers to reveal how they wanted the saga to turn out. The verdict, as headlined on 4 January, was 'Give him the boot Deirdre!'. 'That's the overwhelming verdict of soap fans who phoned our special hotline on canoodling Ken. And it wasn't just the women who wanted to see him suffer. More than THREE times as many men were on Deirdre's side as those who called in to say she should forgive him.' The poll results even warranted mention in the *Daily Star*'s leader column.

The Glasgow *Daily Record* revealed to its readers on 5 January that they would have to prepare themselves for a Ken and Wendy bedroom scene. 'I wish I had gone on a diet before the scene was shot,' William Roache told the paper, 'because my weight was really embarrassing. I don't view myself as a sex symbol but that made me realise I'm overweight.' Three days later, viewers saw the bedroom scene, and London *Evening Standard* critic Jaci Stephen wrote, 'We have now discovered that not only can Wendy afford silk dressing gowns and a flat bigger than the rest of Coronation Street put together (pretty good on a temp's salary), she can afford to have her bedding laundered before, after and, it seems, during each coital encounter. It also seems that Ken makes love with his trousers on.'

Advice was soon filling newspaper columns everywhere. *Manchester Evening News* columnist Laura Marcus asserted 'Mistresses are losers'. 'Statistically very few married men ever leave their wives for mistresses. The real Ken Barlows of this

◄ *Ken Barlow's third marriage crumbles when he falls for Wendy Crozier*

▼ *Tracy Barlow faces up to losing a second father*

world stay with Deirdre, they don't give up hearth and home for the likes of Wendy.' The paper also spoke to two mistresses, both of whom referred to the emotional needs that were satisfied by taking another woman's husband. Things were beginning to get heavy!

The *Daily Express*, on 11 January 1990, focused on 'How the children cope'. As Tracy Barlow's bewilderment was changing to anger with her father, the paper declared, 'Whether we side with Deirdre, the wife, alone and miserable, or the devoted mistress, Wendy, we must agree that the real victim is 12-year-old Tracy.' A lecturer in development psychology was asked for his professional verdict.

One of the few real anti-Deirdre lines came from Celia Brayfield in *7 Days*, the *Sunday Telegraph* magazine, on 14 January. 'Ken Barlow has been the archetypal nice guy in Hush Puppies for decades,' she wrote. 'His fundamental honesty and gentleness have brought him so much grief that we feel he deserves a bit of illicit bliss. Deirdre has always been a sensible woman with the sensuality of a candlewick bedspread. There is a basic lack of poetry about her which inspires hostility. We feel she has brought this misery on herself.'

A day later, the *Daily Star* was reporting that the 'love-rift between Ken and Deirdre Barlow is helping to SAVE real marriages'. A marriage guidance counsellor told the paper,

'The *Street*'s producers have obviously done a great deal of research into marriage breakdown. They have got the emotional side of a split-up just right. It is going to make couples think twice before separating – especially if children are involved.'

The paper followed this a day later with a calculation of how much the split would cost Ken and Deirdre financially. A solicitor offered advice to each separately, and a financial expert suggested making new wills, insuring their lives to provide for Tracy, and he advised on their tax position: 'Ken has already made a mistake by selling the business before they are legally separated,' said the expert. 'If he had waited, they could have claimed £5,000 each from the sale as exempt from capital gains tax.'

The mood of the nation was echoed in the *Manchester Evening News* on 19 January, under the headline 'We're with you, Deirdre!' Dianne Robinson wrote, 'Readers came out firmly behind *Coronation Street*'s wronged wife when we asked what they thought of Ken Barlow's affair with another woman. Kick him out was the overwhelming verdict from the many readers who wrote in.' Ken finally ditched Wendy but he knew Deirdre would not be waiting for him with open arms. When staunch, reliable Ken, an evergreen in the *Street*, went off the rails, he committed a sin worse than being boring, and few viewers were likely to forgive him.

THEY ALSO SERVED

Many actors and actresses who appeared in *Coronation Street* have since gone on to fame elsewhere. Ben Kingsley played Roy Jenkins, who, with a friend, set out to date Irma and Valerie Barlow in the Sixties, long before his stardom in *Gandhi*. Mary Tamm played the Ogdens' daughter-in-law Pauline in 1973, a year before starring in the film *The Odessa File*. Joanna Lumley played headmaster's daughter Elaine Perkins, with whom Ken Barlow was smitten in 1973. Angela Douglas played snake charmer Eunice Bond, otherwise 'La Composita', a girlfriend of Dennis Tanner in the Sixties.

David Jones, who played Ena Sharples's grandson Colin Lomax in an episode in 1961,

later became one of the pop group The Monkees. Peter Noone, who was seen as Len Fairclough's son Stanley in the same year, became famous in the pop world with Herman's Hermits. Michael Ball played Malcolm Nuttall, a tennis-playing friend of Michelle Robinson, Kevin Webster's girlfriend at the time, before becoming the star of Andrew Lloyd Webber's musical *Aspects of Love*.

Comedian Stan Stennett played Hilda Ogden's brother, chip shop owner Norman Crabtree, Max Wall played Harry Payne, a friend of Elsie Tanner, Bill Maynard played song agent Mickey Malone, to whom Stan Ogden sold some of Ena's compositions as his own work, and Leonard Sachs, chairman

▲ *Before starring as Ghandi, Ben Kingsley played smooth-talking Ron Jenkins, who chatted up Irma Barlow*

◄ *Bill Maynard played song agent Micky Malone before fame in* Oh No It's Selwyn Froggitt

of *The Good Old Days* TV show, played Sir Julius Berlin, owner of the Warehouse.

Prunella Scales, of *After Henry*, played bus conductress Eileen Hughes, Mollie Sugden was seen as Nellie Harvey, landlady of the Laughing Donkey, and Mollie's husband, William Moore, who starred with her in *My Husband and I*, appeared as Cyril Turpin, Betty's husband.

Stephanie Turner, star of *Juliet Bravo*, played a member of a girls' pipe band involved with Dennis Tanner in 1967. Peter Childs, Sgt Rycott in *Minder*, played businessman Frank Tyler, who wanted to buy some shirts from Jack Duckworth in 1984. Martin Shaw, of *The Professionals*, played Robert Croft, leader of a hippie commune of squatters who moved into No 11 in 1968. Michael Elphick, of *Boon*, played landlord's son Douglas Wormald, who tried to buy the Kabin in 1974, and David Daker, also in *Boon*, played Gordon Lewis, relief manager at the Rovers in the Eighties.

Some went into other soaps after *Coronation Street*. Alan Rothwell, who was in the first episode as Ken Barlow's brother David, later became Nicholas Black in *Brookside*. Peter Dean, who played lorry driver Fangio Bateman – he pinched Gail Tilsley's bottom in 1980 – became Pete Beale in *EastEnders*. Comedian Stan Stennett, who played Hilda Ogden's brother, chip shop owner Norman Crabtree, became Sid Hopper in *Crossroads*. Tony Anholt, who played David Law, crooked boss of a model agency in 1975, later became Charles Frere in *Howard's Way*, and Patricia Shakesby, who was Ken Barlow's girlfriend Susan Cunningham in the first episode, became Polly Urquhart in the nautical soap. Diana Davies, who played Maggie Clegg's assistant Norma Ford in the corner shop in 1972, became Mrs Bates in *Emmerdale*, and Arthur Pentelow who in 1968 played park-keeper George Greenwood, a friend of Hilda Ogden, became Henry Wilks in the farming serial.

The late Richard Beckinsale played a police constable in 1969, before starring in *Rising Damp* and *Porridge*. Paul Shane, seen as Frank Draper of the post office in 1979, went on to star in *Hi-de-Hi!* Gilly Coman, seen as stripper Sugar La Marr at Fred Gee's stag night in 1981, became Aveline in *Bread*, and Arthur Lowe, as shopkeeper Leonard Swindley, who was jilted by Emily Nugent, became Capt Mainwaring in *Dad's Army*. Kenneth Cope, who played Minnie Caldwell's lodger Jed Stone, went on to become the ghostly half of *Randall and Hopkirk (Deceased)*.

▲ *Celebrated comedy actress Prunella Scales was bus conductress Eileen Hughes, pictured with Harry Hewitt*

◄ Professionals *star Martin Shaw was hippie commune leader Robert Croft (seated, right)*

HATCH

The *Street* welcomed its first new baby in June 1961, when Elsie Tanner's daughter, Linda, wife of Ivan Cheveski, gave birth to son Paul, who weighed in at 7lb 2½oz. Births have usually brought an extra air of happiness to street residents, none more so than when Ken and Valerie Barlow had twins Susan and Peter in 1965.

Less happy was Brian Tilsley on the arrival of daughter Sarah in 1988 after wife Gail had had an affair with his Australian cousin Ian Latimer. A blood test subsequently proved that Latimer could not be the father, but it did not stop Brian and Gail divorcing.

◄*August 1962: Harry and Concepta Hewitt dote on their newly born son Christopher, whose subsequent kidnap attracted the programme's biggest audience to that date*

►*April 1965: Happier times for Ken Barlow as he and first wife Valerie play with twins Peter and Susan. Valerie's subsequent death meant the twins were brought up in Glasgow*

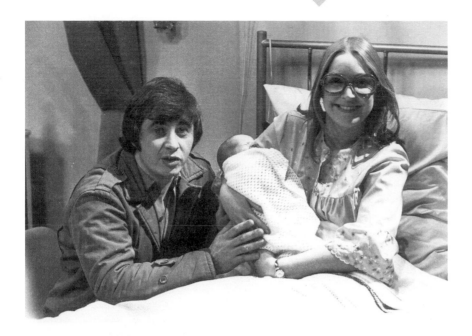

◀ *January 1977: It's a baby girl for Ray and Deirdre Langton. They call her Tracy*

▼ *December 1980: Proud Mum Gail Tilsley hugs 7lb 2oz son Nicky*

MATCH

Weddings are always guaranteed to boost viewing figures. The *Street*'s most popular was in September 1967, when Steve and Elsie Tanner married. Ken and Deirdre Barlow's 1981 wedding was a bigger TV audience-puller than the Prince and Princess of Wales's real-life wedding two days later.

The programme's first couple to tie the knot were Gordon Davies and Joan Walker, daughter of Rovers landlord and landlady Jack and Annie. Ken Barlow has wed three times, as have Alf Roberts and Elsie Tanner, who were already married when they entered the serial. Emily Bishop has married twice, but found her second husband to be a bigamist.

▲ *March 1969; One of the* Street's *weddings that never was. Lucille Hewitt tries on her wedding dress, but fiancé Gordon Clegg arrives to call off the wedding.*

▲ *March 1961: Rovers Return landlord Jack Walker prepares to give away daughter Joan at her wedding to teacher Gordon Davies. The couple move to Derby*

▲ July 1981: It's specs off for Deirdre Langton as she marries Ken Barlow at All Saints Church. Ken adopts Deirdre's daughter, Tracy

▲ September 1967: Steve and Elsie Tanner cut the cake after their wedding in Warrington, near his air base

► May 1986: Another doomed marriage. Susan Barlow weds Mike Baldwin, her father's arch enemy after his affair with Deirdre. Mike and Susan divorce after she becomes pregnant and has an abortion

DESPATCH

Deaths are always a sad occasion, but the *Street* has had more than its fair share of violent endings. Ken Barlow's first wife, Valerie, was fatally electrocuted by a faulty hairdryer plug, Ernest Bishop was shot in a wages snatch and Brian Tilsley came to an untimely end when he was knifed outside a nightclub.

The *Street*'s first death was May Hardman. When Martha Longhurst passed away in the Rovers Snug in 1964, her death attracted more viewers than the General Election night coverage. More recently, there was particular sadness at the deaths of Albert Tatlock, Stan Ogden and Bert Tilsley.

◄ *New Year's Eve 1960: May Hardman collapses from a heart attack at her home, No. 13*

▼ *May 1964: A heart attack also claims Martha Longhurst, who is laid to rest after her death in the pub*

▶ *January 1978: Ernest Bishop meets a violent end, fatally shot in a wages snatch at the warehouse. He dies on the operating table*

◀ *July 1980: Renee Roberts is taken from the wreckage of her car after being hit by a lorry*

▶ *December 1989: Rita Fairclough's cheating ex-lover Alan Bradley is instantly killed when struck by a Blackpool tram*

Violet Carson

When Violet Carson decided to 'have a go' at the part of Ena Sharples at the age of sixty-two, her attitude typified that of most of the cast. She treated it like a one-off play: six weeks' promised work and then on to something new. Five weeks after the opening night, however, one newspaper journalist ventured to suggest that Ena was already better known than the Prime Minister. Stardom had claimed the whole cast for its own.

Vi's home town of Blackpool pressed her into service and asked her to switch on their 500,000 illuminations. The craggy contours of her face were moulded in wax in Madame Tussaud's, and a Violet Carson rose turned up at garden centres. In October 1965, she was summoned to Buckingham Palace to receive the OBE and told by the Queen, 'I am a most ardent fan of yours.'

Violet was an educated, well-spoken Lancashire actress who turned into TV's most famous harridan via a quick-change act that would have impressed Paul Daniels. Ena was created in seconds, courtesy of jamming three hairnets firmly over Violet's immaculately coiffeured silver-grey hair. Just as speedily, and conveniently for Violet, she could bring about the same transformation in reverse with a quick flick of her comb. 'I have never been haunted by Ena,' she said. 'I have always been able to leave her behind the moment I closed the dressing-room door.'

She was a warm, intelligent actress who was a connoisseur of good taste and moral values. She brooked no nonsense from people. Even television directors on the studio floor would get it in the neck if she thought they were waffling, fussing around

her or wasting her time. She had strong views on the way sex dominates certain areas of the media and public discussion. 'I think sex is an absolute bloody bore,' she told journalists. 'Everything seems to be equated with sex, and I'm sick and tired of it. Why don't they leave it where it should be – up in the bedroom?' Violet's homespun words of wisdom to young girls were equally forthright: 'Don't expect too much out of life. Give as much as you can and listen to what your mother says.'

Born in a real Coronation Street-type house in German Street, Manchester, Violet was the daughter of a flour miller. Her mother was a fine amateur singer. She was introduced to music almost as soon as she could walk. She was not quite three when her mother sat her down at the piano for her first lesson. By the time she was ten, she was an able pianist. Her chance to earn a living at her hobby came unexpectedly. 'My sister's violin teacher was leader of the orchestra at the old Market Street cinema in Manchester in the days of silent movies,' recalled Violet. 'They needed a relief pianist in a hurry and I got the call – I was petrified with fright. I put on my best green dress and tied ribbons in my pigtails, and set off with my music. I stayed for two wonderful years. You had to be able to do everything from symphonies to "chase" music for Westerns.'

Violet married her sweetheart, road contractor George Peplow, in 1926 in Manchester Cathedral, where she had been christened 28 years earlier. George had been her one and only beau, and she was stunned when he died two years later. Many years after, Violet explained, 'I was a one-man girl. I met him, loved him, and lost him, and wanted no one else.'

After she was widowed, Violet went back to her music, playing for dinners, concerts and musical evenings. She made her first radio broadcast at the BBC's Manchester studios and soon became one of Britain's best-known radio voices, singing everything from Lancashire comic songs in the Stanley Holloway manner to operatic arias. During World War Two, she travelled all over the country, entertaining the troops. Back in

◀ *Violet Carson was known to friends as 'The Duchess'*

▼ *Ena Sharples, 'a hag in a hairnet'*

Civvy Street, she became the nation's favourite auntie – 'Auntie Vi' of BBC radio's *Children's Hour*. Next came her radio partnership with Wilfred Pickles, playing the piano for his national networked quiz *Have a Go*. She was a popular *Woman's Hour* contributor and graduated to drama. 'I did dozens of radio plays – in fact, I've done everything on BBC radio bar reading the news and giving the Epilogue,' said Violet.

When *Coronation Street* came along, she was already 62. She launched Ena Sharples on screen with a flint-hard torrent of words that would have blunted Shakespeare's quill:

ENA to Florrie Lindley: 'Are you a widder woman?'
FLORRIE: 'Well, yes.'
ENA: 'What's yer place of worship?'
FLORRIE: 'Well, I don't really do very much about it.'
ENA (nodding wisely): 'Oh, yes, C of E.'
ENA: 'Where yer being buried?'
FLORRIE: 'I've not given it much thought.'
ENA: 'Well, you should. But think on you don't go to that crematorium. As the coffin rolls away, they play Moonlight and Roses *. . . I'm rolling away to* Crimond.'

Ena's mission in life was to confront authority and deflate humbugs, but there was a softer side to her, too. She played the church harmonium like an angel and was unshakeably loyal to her friends. There was even a kind word for sworn enemy Elsie Tanner, with whom she had many an 'upper and downer' about Elsie's 'fancy men'. But, when Elsie was suicidally low, Ena lent a friendly ear.

After Violet's retirement from the serial because of ill health, she said, 'When I went into television I thought they wanted glamour, but what they wanted was a hag in a hairnet – and I became that for twenty years. Having said that, I loved the old girl. She pontificated, preached, irritated and annoyed, but she was pure gold. A lady who minded her manners and everybody else's business. I am a very lucky woman. I have been offered all the riches a woman could be offered and I hope I have made the most of them.'

Cruising was one of her great private pastimes, with her widowed sister Nellie. Unknown to her fans, Violet was always known to friends as 'The Duchess'. 'I have been a duchess all my life – I have probably got a ramrod up my back,' she said. She spent her final years in her little seaside bungalow near Blackpool, surrounded by the rose-filled garden that she loved. Sadly, she was not well enough to join the programme's 2,000th episode champagne celebrations at the Granada TV Centre in June 1980. Violet Carson died in December 1983, aged 85.

ELSIE TANNER

Pat Phoenix

Pat Phoenix, the 'working man's Raquel Welch', sent such a shiver through the nation's menfolk that she received four marriage proposals a week. What was it that made three-times-married Elsie Tanner so appealing? She shocked and wowed male viewers in the less liberated Sixties with her daring cleavage and her just-got-out-of-bed look.

But success has its drawbacks. 'I reached the point where I couldn't go out without being recognised,' said Pat. 'It's a terrific strain because everyone expects me to be-have like Elsie. They ply me with gin and tonics, but my tipple is soda water.'

At the start of *Coronation Street*, Elsie was knee-deep in parental problems, trying to sort out her likeable but wayward son Dennis, and the marital problems of daugh-ter Linda who was married to the tempestu-ous Czech, Ivan Cheveski. Things looked brighter for her when her wartime sweet-heart, US Army Master Sergeant Steve Tanner, romanced her down the aisle in 1967. But they soon realised that they were trying to live a dream. They drifted apart and Steve died a year later, murdered by a fel-low-soldier.

Elsie turned down two marriage proposals from her old friend Len Fairclough before falling for Geordie businessman Alan Howard. Unfortunately, it turned out to be third time unlucky for the siren of soap. As Howard turned to drink, another Tanner marriage foundered. 'In all, there were 23 accountable fellas – lovers, husbands, boy-friends – in Elsie's 22-year run in the pro-gramme. And maybe a few more that the scriptwriters never told us about.'

Irish-born Pat Phoenix was brought up in

Manchester by her mother, a beautiful, natural redhead called Anna Maria Josephine Noonan. Her stepfather told her she'd never make an actress but, with that determined streak that ultimately took her to the top, she defied him and managed to land a small part in a radio play while still at school. Regular work followed through BBC radio's *Children's Hour*. Although her first full-time job was working as a filing clerk for the then Manchester Corporation, she followed her first love as best she could by joining the Manchester Arts Group and Shakespearian Society.

Her big chance came when she managed to break into repertory theatre. Ironically, it was television that first damaged her theatri-cal career. Dozens of small repertory com-panies went to the wall as 'the box' captured traditional theatre audiences. Pat was advised to move to London where, she was confident, she would take the capital by storm. 'I did,' she recalled, 'or at least I took the London Labour Exchange by storm.' A seven-year lean period followed in which she struggled to eek out a living. Appearances in horror films such as *Blood of the Vampire* and *Jack the Ripper* were by necessity rather than choice. In the summer of 1960, she returned to Manchester, exhausted and all but defeated. She was within a whisker of giving up acting. 'Well, it seemed to have given me up,' she said years later.

It was Elsie Tanner who rescued her from oblivion. Television success transformed both her financial status and her outlook on life. From then on, as if to compensate for the lean years, Pat seemed determined to live the good life. In 1967, she moved to a house in Disley, Cheshire. Set in several acres, it had a ballroom and a billiards room, and Pat's parties became famous. She was a very generous person and it was 'open house' to all.

In 1972, she married actor Alan Browning, her third screen husband, who had joined the cast as Alan Howard. It was a glitzy showbusiness wedding with toppers and tails, Pat dressed in mink, with horse-drawn carriages to the church. A year later, Pat and Alan left *Coronation Street* to try their luck with a 43-week theatre revival of the Victorian melodrama *Gaslight*. Tragically, Alan Browning died in 1979, but the couple had already split up.

There was jubilation from her fans when Pat rejoined the *Street* cast in 1976. 'It's got nothing to do with the money,' she said. 'This is where my friends arc. I'm home again.'

Some time after Alan Browning's death, Pat sought the companionship of a very old friend, actor Tony Booth – known to millions as Alf Garnett's 'Scouse git' son-in-law in *Till Death Us Do Part*. Thcy had shared the same stage together 23 years earlier as struggling actors.

Pat, who was the darling of Fleet Street television writers, hit the headlincs again in 1983 with her surprise decision to quit thc *Street* for good. She did a variety of work after that, and joked about getting her pension's bus pass on her sixtieth birthday. She played agony aunt on TV-am and local radio. She even landed a starring role as a brassy seaside landlady in an ITV comedy series, *Constant Hot Water*.

Both friends and fans were devastated in 1986, when doctors confirmed that she was suffering from incurable lung cancer, the legacy of smoking sixty cigarettes a day for most of her adult life. Typically, Pat fought it with style and humour. She gave a number of press conferences in which she appeared clutching teddy bears and soft toys from adoring fans, but the cancer had sapped even her enormous grit and strength. There was a final showbiz flourish yet to come, however. She married Tony Booth in a moving ceremony in hospital. Via the press, she told her public, 'Thank you very much, loves, and ta-ra.'

There is a sad postscript to the Pat Phoenix story. In May 1989, 300 items of Pat's treasured possessions went under the auctioneer's hammer. They included furniture, jewellery, even her collection of cuddly teddy bears. But it wasn't the *objets d'art* or even mink fur coat, hand-embroidered with her name, that touched the heart strings. It was little things that you knew she cared about, such as the boxes of books autographed on the fly-leaves that she probably read at rehearsals while waiting to be called on set.

A dozen scrapbooks of press cuttings and photographs spanning two decades as a soap-opera superstar seemed most poignant. There were accounts of her all-conquering trip to Australia, where she was mobbed by adoring fans. The items were put up for sale by Tony Booth, who shared Pat's olde worlde cottage at Hollingsworth, Derbyshire, before she died.

▶ *Elsie earns extra money modelling for the School of Design*

Doris Speed *AND* Arthur Leslie

AS ANNIE AND JACK WALKER

Although Doris Speed continued in *Coronation Street* for thirteen years after the sudden death of Arthur Leslie in 1970, it is logical to consider them together as the first great 'double act' in the programme, who featured in some of the best storylines of the first decade. Doris and Arthur, like their characters Jack and Annie Walker – first licensees of the Rovers Return – were chalk and cheese. They had a wonderful working relationship, but Arthur was placid and easy-going, while Doris, who played toffee-nosed Annie to perfection, was a very independent woman who was lively, outspoken and full of fun. Both were veterans of the business when they joined the *Street* at its start, in December 1960. Arthur was 60 and Doris was 61 – an unbelievable 84 when she left the programme in 1983. Television stardom obviously held no terrors for them.

Arthur Leslie was born in a trunk – his actor-parents were on tour in Newark, Nottinghamshire, when he was conceived in 1910. He worked solely in live theatre until he was sixty, spending most of his theatrical career in Lancashire. He played in repertory in Wigan for eleven seasons and ran his own company at the Theatre Royal, Leigh, for two years. One of life's true gentlemen, nothing seemed to rattle him. There was more than a hint of Arthur in Jack Walker, who, when bullied or needled by his social-climbing wife, merely sighed, 'Eee, Annie, luv!' It became his catchphrase. As Annie tried to exercise her social superiority over the 'hoi polloi', Jack stoically kept a diplomatic silence. Just occasionally, however, the worm turned. When Jack decided to put his foot down, one firm word was enough to topple Annie from her lofty perch and reduce her to tearful silence. In important matters, he was the boss.

Arthur Leslie and Doris Speed forged a partnership that could have run and run, and it was a devastating blow to close friends and the production team when he died suddenly on holiday in 1970. Hundreds of fans flocked to his funeral in Blackpool to pay tribute. The scriptwriters were left with a huge gap to fill and it was ultimately decided that Annie Walker should soldier on alone, which she did for another 13 years, with Jack's photograph always prominently placed on her sideboard.

Like Arthur Leslie, Doris Speed was practically born in a theatre. Her mum and dad, George and Ada Speed, were a struggling music-hall act, on tour when she was born. She made her debut in the family act when she was three. Flaxen-haired Doris toddled on in her nightdress, carrying a candle and singing a song about a golliwog. At five, she played the velvet-suited child, the Prince of Rome, in a Victorian melodrama called *The Royal Divorce*. Doris served a long apprenticeship in rep, musical comedy, and radio, before she made her television debut as the trolley-pushing tea lady in an early Granada TV drama series called *Skyport*.

It was only when tabloid newspaper revelations in 1983 revealed that she was an incredible 84 years old, that Granada discovered she had retired from one job as an office worker before she broke back into regular acting again, courtesy of *Coronation Street*. Doris herself admits that there was a serious lull between acting spells. 'Until I got into *Coronation Street*, I was convinced that I was going to be another theatrical has-been,' she said. 'It revived and revitalised my whole career.'

Even then, she had no way of weighing the scale of the TV role that awaited her. She was doing a play at Bristol and, when the call came to audition, she turned Granada down twice, until her agent warned her that she would regret it all her life if she didn't turn up. What Doris didn't know was that Tony Warren had written the role of Annie specially for her. He recalled her work in a BBC radio *Children's Hour* play they once did together and he was impressed.

Annie Walker of the withering look and Lady Bracknell manner was based, according to Doris, on her Auntie Bessie, who used to lead family charades at Christmas – and woe betide those who didn't take them seriously. What a contrast. There was no such side to Doris at all. A life-long socialist, she had no obvious trappings of wealth beyond a much loved fur coat. She didn't run a car, holiday in exotic places or live in a mansion. She just chose to carry on living modestly in her comfortable Manchester suburban semi-detached house where she lived with her elderly mother, Ada.

Ada was a mistress of the cutting remark and could take Doris down a peg or two in a trice, just in case national TV fame might have gone to her head. She once told Doris, 'I am 87 years of age, but thank God I never looked as old as you did on TV tonight!' Doris refused to speak to her for a week after that.

Great Annie Walker storylines included the Jubilee pageant in June 1977, when Annie played Elizabeth I to Ena Sharples's Queen Victoria in a tableau called 'Britain Through the Ages'. There she was, holding centre stage on the brewery float but, unfortunately, Stan Ogden had left the lorry's lights on all night and the battery was flat. The result was an undignified scramble to the carnival assembly point in the park. Mrs Walker was most definitely not amused.

Annie's other abomination was coarseness or unseemly behaviour in the bar of the Rovers, despite the fact that it was clearly a working-class pub. Len Fairclough, Stan Ogden, Eddie Yeats and the like all felt the rough edge of her tongue from time to time. Ken Barlow, on the other hand, a consumer of gentlemanly half-pints of beer and an 'intellectual' in Annie's eyes because he was a teacher, was eternally welcome. Although she once lost a local council election to Len Fairclough on the toss of a coin, Annie's crowning moment was when she became Mayoress of Weatherfield at the invitation of Alf Roberts, a Mayor 'between wives' at the time. She took to it as if to the manor born.

Certainly, Annie Walker was one of the great pillars on which *Coronation Street* was founded, and there was another dilemma for the writers when Doris Speed finally retired through ill health in 1983. Fleet Street were the culprits here. A national newspaper ran a revelatory story about her age, complete with a photocopy of her birth certificate. Even Granada staff were amazed – they thought she was only in her mid-seventies. The shock was too much for Doris, and she retired gracefully from the serial. Happily, after a long period of convalescence, Doris made a surprise visit to the studios in 1985 to attend *Coronation Street*'s Silver Jubilee celebration party.

Annie Walker, by the way, lives in comfortable retirement with her daughter Joan. Wayward son Billy still turns up in the *Street* from time to time, carrying on the Walker dynasty.

Jack Howarth

Jack Howarth was a star long before *Coronation Street* was first thought of. 'I never experienced hard times,' said the man known to millions as British television's 'Mr Grumpy', Albert Tatlock, the OAP in a threadbare suit and cap. Although Jack completed 24 years and 1,700 TV appearances as Albert, he enjoyed a very successful stage and radio career before that.

Born in Rochdale in 1896, he went to school with Gracie Fields and was a child actor from the age of twelve. His father was a comedian, so it was natural for Jack to follow him into showbusiness. His first job was to sell programmes in the auditorium at a penny each, then he started by playing juvenile leads with Churchill's Minstrels in 1908. During World War One, he served with the Lancashire Fusiliers in France.

It was while he was on tour in Llandudno that he met his wife-to-be, actress Betty Murgatroyd. They were married in 1929 in mid-tour while appearing in Hull in a stage version of *Dracula*. No honeymoon for them – it was business as usual on stage on the night of their wedding. The Howarths made a vow: they would either work together or one would give up a role so that they did not become separated from the other. They celebrated their Golden Wedding in July 1979, after 'fifty glorious years'.

It was Jack's career that took off with Northern repertory, plus feature film cameos such as the part of clogmaker Tubby in Charles Laughton's *Hobson's Choice*. After World War One, he became a stage director for Hamilton Deane, working on the original production of *Frankenstein*. During World War Two, Jack ran a theatre in Colwyn Bay for six years, playing most of the male roles himself because there was a shortage of men. His best-known radio role was the part of Mr Maggs in *Mrs Dale's Diary*, which he played for fourteen years. In a way, the grumpy old Maggs was a forerunner of the Albert Tatlock role.

Hearing of a new Northern TV serial in preparation, Jack asked his agent to pursue the possibility of an opening. Other actors had competed for the Tatlock role, but it was Jack who clinched it. He made the part of the contrary old war veteran his own right from Episode One.

Jack and Albert were poles apart as far as lifestyles were concerned. Generally speaking, Albert wouldn't accept charity and lived a frugal life on his pension, with one exception – he had a weakness for cadging double rums from whomever he could con in the Rovers Return. By contrast, Jack lived in a suite in the four-star Midland Hotel in Manchester while working on the *Street* and relaxed in his tasteful bungalow on the Welsh coast at weekends. He and Betty also travelled widely to swish resorts such as Monte Carlo. To balance that, he was a tireless worker for charity, and the Spastics Society in particular.

Jack died in 1984. His last appearance in the programme was on Wednesday, 2 January, that year. Albert Tatlock died while staying with his daughter Beattie in Cumberland Close, Weatherfield.

Peter Adamson

A S
LEN FAIRCLOUGH

Len Fairclough was the 'macho man' of *Coronation Street* for 23 years. Men liked his bravado and comradeship, and women liked his caveman line in small-talk and his reckless disregard for convention. At his peak in the Sixties, he was a magnetic character enjoyed by millions.

When he arrived in Weatherfield in 1961, his first marriage to Nellie Briggs was already on the rocks, and it wasn't long before Mrs Fairclough, plus son, disappeared with an insurance salesman. Len had a few liaisons in his time. He was always sweet on Elsie Tanner, but she would never agree to marry him.

His conquests included then barmaid Bet Lynch, with whom he had a torrid affair, but it was Rita Littlewood who finally took his eye. She was a kindred spirit, and it was no surprise when they threw in their lot together. Len was a big shot by now – local councillor and owner of his own plumbing and building business. Just when life seemed to be turning sweet for Mr and Mrs Fairclough, news came of a tragic car crash in December 1983. Len had died at the wheel as his car hit a bridge, while driving back from a visit to see a secret girlfriend.

Liverpool-born Peter Adamson started his working life as a commercial artist, indulging his first love, the stage, in the evenings as an amateur. At the age of nineteen he won a place at the London Academy of Music and Dramatic Art. He lasted just two months – the high spirited Peter simply refused to take the lessons seriously.

Changing tack, he determined to break into theatre the hard way as an 'extra' and bit-part actor. His big break came when a theatre in Sale, Cheshire, offered him a job back in the North. In 1949, he joined the Frank H. Fortescue Players at Bury as a stage manager. In 1956, soon after ITV started, Peter Adamson got a job as a comedy host on a TV record show. His first taste of TV drama was in Granada's early series *Skyport* and *Knight Errant*.

He had been out of regular work for something like three months when news of Granada's new baby, *Coronation Street*, filtered through to him. When his big chance came, he was asked to read for the roles of Dennis Tanner and Ken Barlow but was considered to be of too mature a build, to put it politely, but, three months after the programme launched, Peter was recruited to play the small part of Len Fairclough.

Public reaction was mixed. Disturbed viewers wrote in asking Granada to drop the loud-mouthed, hard-drinking bully. Other people reacted differently, such as the men in the street who offered Adamson a real-life scrap, just to find out how tough he really was. At the time, Peter was a fairly beefy specimen who, with his Liverpool upbringing, might well have been able to give a good account of himself in a fight, but he chose to take the least line of resistance and settled for a disguise – cloth cap and dark glasses.

When Len moved into No 9 Coronation Street, Peter knew he had found fame and job security at last. He stayed in the *Street* until 1983.

Bernard Youens

STAN OGDEN

Stan Ogden was the boozy, work-shy layabout who was the uncrowned king of the 'non-working' classes and the darling of millions for twenty years, but he was the creation of a beautifully spoken, velvet-voiced actor–TV announcer who was the complete antithesis of 'Hilda Ogden's cross', as producer Harry Kershaw used to call 'Big Oggy'. Bernard Youens began his stage career as assistant stage manager at the Players' Theatre, Newcastle upon Tyne, while still in his teens. He met and married his wife Edna, a ballet dancer, when he was just eighteen.

Bernard worked in repertory theatres all over Britain before being called up in 1940. He served in the 1st Battalion, the Loyals Regiment, and saw service in North Africa, Egypt and Anzio. After being demobbed in 1946, he returned to the theatre, then joined Granada TV in 1956 as a continuity announcer, working in tandem with the late Ray Moore, destined to become a household name as a Radio 2 presenter. Soon, Bernard was acting in early Granada drama series such as *Knight Errant* and *Shadow Squad*.

Bernard had almost quit the business at one point, becoming landlord of a run-down Manchester public house. There were fist-fights every Saturday night and, eventually, the unruly regulars forced him to quit. Of necessity, he took a job as a bread salesman. After that, he became a building site labourer to earn a few quid. Bernard and Edna had another bash at running a pub near Preston, before the announcer's job cropped up at the Granada TV Centre.

In one of those quirky little twists of fate that can make or break an actor's career, Bernard actually turned down the chance to audition for the original *Street* cast in 1960. He had had so many ups and downs in life that, with five children to feed, he put greater store by the security of his staff announcer's job. His great love was theatre, but it rarely paid the bills.

In 1961, after *Coronation Street* had become a nationwide hit, he was kicking himself that he had missed out on an even bigger opportunity. Fate stepped in when the production team cast around for new recruits in 1964. He forged a partnership with Jean Alexander that was a screen hit from the off. Bernard's Hardy to Jean's Laurel, it has been suggested. Stan was a kind of Lancashire version of Andy Capp whose mission in life was to make a quick quid for the minimum of effort. From the moment he uttered his first line, 'A pint of mild and twenty fags, missus,' Bernard had crossed the bridge from theatrical obscurity to national television fame. 'He is my creation and I am proud of him,' said Bernard, who was later toasted by members of the Stan Ogden Appreciation Society of Newton Abbot, who dubbed their TV favourite 'the greatest living Englishman'.

One piece of Ogden arch-trickery in particular massages the funny bones of millions. When Stan tripped over a paving stone, injuring his big toe, he sued the local authority for compensation. It started a rash of real-life 'copycat' claims that infuriated many a local alderman and town clerk.

Life for Stan Ogden and Bernard Youens carried on serenely until the late Seventies, when Bernard was suddenly struck down by a series of heart attacks, followed by two strokes, which left his speech badly impaired – a double tragedy for a man who had a superb broadcasting voice, but Bernard wasn't finished yet. He bravely refused to give up acting and engaged a speech therapist to teach him how to speak again.

His screen burden was lightened considerably by the emergence of the Ogdens' new lodger, Eddie Yeats, played by Geoffrey Hughes. Roly-poly Eddie took over Stan's window-cleaning round, with Oggy as a kind of sleeping partner. In reality, Jean Alexander and Geoffrey Hughes began to shoulder the storyline and main dialogue, carrying Bernard on to new heights of popularity with his adoring public. He had always

been one of the hardest working actors in the show.

Unfortunately, a new health problem struck. For nearly twenty years, he had struggled with arthritis of the knees and neck and, as the condition became more critical, it restricted his movements on set. His condition worsened and, in a major setback, he had to have his left leg amputated when surgeons found gangrene. Bernard died in hospital in April 1984, aged 69.

Compelled to write Stan Ogden out of the serial, the scriptwriters had him die in hospital. A great double-act had taken its final curtain. Jean Alexander paid fitting tribute: 'I shall miss him more than I can say. We shared a friendship and a twenty-year partnership which, in its way, made television history. His was a marvellous screen creation and he will be deeply missed by millions.'

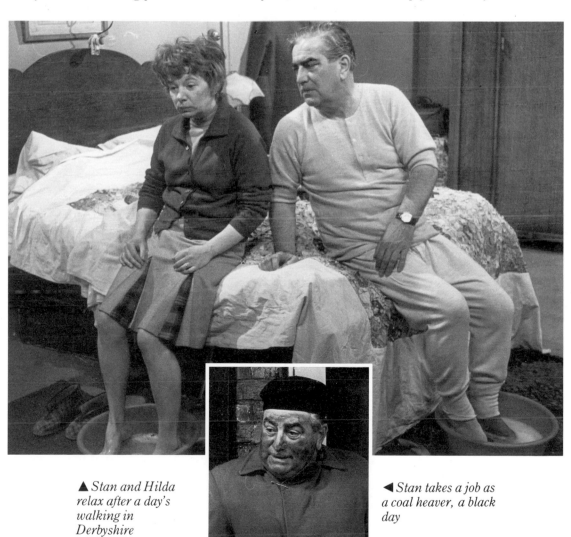

▲ *Stan and Hilda relax after a day's walking in Derbyshire*

◄ *Stan takes a job as a coal heaver, a black day*

Jean Alexander

AS
HILDA OGDEN

Jean Alexander's exit from *Coronation Street* at Christmas 1987 was a real shock to the nation. It came without warning or apparent cause. There had been no bouts of ill health or outbursts of histrionics, which heralded some cast departures. The woman known to millions as 'Our Hilda' just quietly announced that, after 23 years of commuting between her Southport home and Granada's Manchester studios, she had simply had enough. 'I've worked hard all my life since 1945,' she told the press, 'and it's time to put my feet up.'

Jean Alexander, born in Liverpool, began her working life as a library assistant, but gave up her job to try her hand at her first love, acting, and joined the Macclesfield-based Adelphi Guild Theatre. To gain further experience, she joined repertory companies in Southport, Oldham and York. She moved to London, making one-off TV appearances in series such as *Z-Cars*, before joining the cast of *Coronation Street* in June 1964.

Like Violet Carson's instant Ena Sharples hairnet transformation, Jean Alexander could become Hilda in a trice. The voice

went up three octaves, Olive Oyl style, and a turban plus three strategically placed hair rollers completed the visual magic. The finishing touch was her now legendary, old-fashioned, blue-and-yellow wrap-round pinny. 'It was donkeys' years old,' said Jean, 'but it seemed to fascinate viewers, who used to write in in droves to see where they could buy one similar.'

Stripped of Hilda's 'uniform', and with a brush flicked quickly through her neatly styled red hair, she became the softly spoken, very private woman who could walk round a crowded city-centre store unrecognised. When she was occasionally spotted, revealed Jean, people tended to say either, 'Oh, it's our Hilda!' or approach her from behind, punch her in the back and shriek with laughter.

In their heyday in the Sixties and Seventies, Stan and Hilda Ogden scaled heights of comedy rarely seen in a British soap before.

Originally conceived by the writers as a fat oaf and his nagging wife, Jean and the late Bernard Youens decided, instead, to play Stan and Hilda more 'Andy Cap and Flo' style, letting a chink of real affection show between the cracks occasionally. The result was pure pathos, which at times reduced viewers to tears.

Jean developed a number of mannerisms for the character. There were Hilda's constantly dangling fag and Charlie Chaplin walk. Between beavering away industriously to pay the bills, Hilda was an ardent fortune-teller who loved to read the tea-leaves. She enjoyed a light ale and kept a beady eye on the world from behind the curtains of No 13 Coronation Street. Hilda's big moment came when she and Stan won a 'second honeymoon' prize at a posh hotel. As she basked in the luxuries and comfort of Room 504, and Stan got tiddly on champagne, she trilled the Forties song *In Room 504*.

Her pride and joy in her poorly furnished house were the painted 'muriel' on her living-room wall and her china ducks – presented to Jean later as a parting gift from the production team.

Modest Jean's performance had now captivated people to such a degree that she was voted the fourth most popular female in Britain, after the Queen, the Queen Mother, and the Princess of Wales. The late Poet Laureate Sir John Betjeman, playwright Willis Hall and TV personalities such as Russell Harty and Michael Parkinson formed The British League for Hilda Ogden. Lord Olivier was president of this appreciation society, which met at London's exclusive Garrick Club – haunt of the theatrical elit.

Official recognition came along in the shape of the Royal Television Society's 1984–5 Best Performance Award, which, fittingly, marked her 21st year as Hilda. Jean's poignant and tender performance during, and after Stan's death, had caught the committee's eye. 'It was the first award I had ever received, and the proudest moment of my life,' Jean said afterwards. Shortly after leaving the *Street*, *TVTimes* readers voted Jean best actress of 1987.

What a pity that her screen partner of twenty years was not around to share the honours. Bernard Youens's death in 1984 had marked the end of an era. Jean was a close friend of Bernard and wife 'Teddy'. 'I miss him more than I can say,' said Jean. 'We never had to discuss a scene or go over a piece of dialogue together. He always turned up word-perfect, just as I did, and we knew exactly how we were going to play it. Working without "Bunny" was like acting without an arm.' But, like Hilda, Jean carried on with dignity. 'I knew that Hilda would never let anyone see her cry – and that's how I played her,' said Jean.

Picture the scene after Stan's death, with Hilda alone in her living-room for the first time. After showing great composure at his funeral she unpacked a parcel of Stan's belongings from hospital, buried her head in her hands and sobbed, in private.

Then, in December 1987, came the moment when Hilda herself disappeared from Britain's top serial. Granada and ITV weren't going to let her go without a touching send-off. The script team and programme controller Steve Morrison scheduled a Christmas Day finale and screen departure that rivalled the Queen's Speech in festive viewing attractions. First came a cliffhanger in which Hilda and Mrs Lowther were victims of a violent burglary. One of them would die – Mrs Lowther drew the short straw. Then, on Christmas Day itself, Hilda put away her pinny and curler, put on her best hat and coat, and went off to keep house for Dr Lowther in an idyllic Derbyshire village.

Will Hilda ever return? The door is still open, and Jean Alexander herself has not ruled out the occasional guest appearance. She remains eternally grateful to Hilda. 'Before I joined *Coronation Street*, I never had more than £15 in the bank in my life,' said Jean. Financial security gave her a taste for ocean cruises and an uncomplicated life in Southport, where she lives alone.

She has not retired from acting, however, and has turned up in the ITV series *Boon*, in a cameo role in *Scandal*, the feature film about the John Profumo affair, as a doddery aunt in two *Last of the Summer Wine* Christmas Specials, and in the ITV children's drama *Woof!*

Jean maintains her decision to quit the *Street* was the right one. 'I have no regrets at all, having worked for over 40 years,' she said. 'I still wake up at 6.30am, but I can turn over and go back to sleep again these days if I want to.'

MEMORABLE MOMENTS 1961–1990
1961

JANUARY

★ Ena Sharples nearly loses her job as care-taker of the Glad Tidings Mission when lay preacher Leonard Swindley sees her drinking milk stout. The stressful confrontation brings on a stroke.

★ Pensioner Albert Tatlock collapses on the floor of his kitchen at No 1 – a victim of high blood pressure – but stubbornly refuses to move in with his daughter Beattie.

★ Elsie Tanner's seaman husband, Arnold, returns unexpectedly from his travels to seek a divorce, and she agrees.

FEBRUARY

★ A fractured gas main is discovered outside in Mawdesley Street and the street's inhabitants are evacuated to the Mission Hall where Ena orders lights out, no smoking, and 'absolutely no funny business'.

★ Frank Barlow is horrified to discover wife Ida has been buying loose covers on hire purchase. He contemplates buying No 3 for £200 but decides it is not worth it.

MARCH

★ Ena misreads a notice outside the town hall and starts a rumour that Coronation Street is to be demolished – a piece of scaremongering for which she is later sent to Coventry by the residents.

★ Joan Walker, daughter of Jack and Annie, marries teetotal vegetarian teacher Gordon Davies and they go to live in Derby.

★ Ken Barlow ends his romance with middle-class Susan Cunningham because their backgrounds are too different.

APRIL

★ Elsie Tanner's daughter Linda and her Polish husband Ivan Cheveski buy No 9 Coronation Street for £565.

★ Ken Barlow, 21, starts an affair with 33 year old university librarian Marion Lund, but later decides she is too old for him.

★ Rovers regulars enjoy a coach outing to Lake Windermere, on which Elsie is accompanied by Det Insp Arthur Dewhurst, whom she helped when she found him beaten up outside her back gate.

★ Widow Alice Burgess agrees to keep house for her brother Harry Hewitt and his wayward daughter Lucille.

MAY

★ Billy Walker, son of Jack and Annie, returns from National Service and takes a job as a mechanic at the Blue Bell garage.

▼ *Ken Barlow's disapproving parents, Frank and Ida, meet girlfriend Marion Lund, 12 years his senior*

▼ *Bus inspector Harry Hewitt finds love for the second time, with Rovers barmaid Concepta Riley*

JUNE
★ Elsie Tanner becomes a grandmother when her daughter Linda gives birth to a 7lb 2½oz son, Paul.
★ Tom Hayes, a salesman of one-armed bandit machines, moves in with his sister Esther at No 5.
★ Emily Nugent closes her baby linen shop and becomes Leonard Swindley's partner in his haberdashery business.

JULY
★ Ken Barlow receives a second class BA honours degree in English and history.
★ Leo and Mario Bonarti open an Italian restaurant in Rosamund Street and Christine Hardman falls for Mario.

AUGUST
★ Florrie Lindley has a £500 win with one of the newly introduced premium bonds.
★ Frank Barlow, father of Ken, is promoted to supervisor at the Post Office.
★ Ken Barlow starts courting Albert Tatlock's niece Valerie, who runs a hairdressing salon in Rosamund Street.

SEPTEMBER
★ The street is shocked when Ida Barlow, wife of Frank and mother of Ken and David, dies under the wheels of a bus.

► *Dennis Tanner restrains mother Elsie as she is provoked by Ena Sharples' sharp tongue*

OCTOBER
★ Rovers regulars take a coach trip to see the Blackpool illuminations, but when it is time to return, Ena is left behind and has to hitch a lift home in a lorry.
★ Widower Harry Hewitt proposes to Concepta Riley, the Rovers' Irish barmaid, and they marry within a month with his daughter Lucille as bridesmaid. Doreen Lostock replaces Concepta at the Rovers.
★ Elsie Tanner is swept off her feet by Petty Officer Bill Gregory, an old navy pal of Len Fairclough.
★ Ken Barlow joins Amalgamated Steel as assistant personnel officer.

NOVEMBER
★ Leonard Swindley faces bankruptcy and is forced to sell his shop to Nicholas Papagopolous, Greek owner of Gamma Garments.
★ Ken Barlow leaves his new job after a row with his boss and becomes a teacher at Bessie Street School.
★ Leonard Swindley finds Ena drinking stout again; she resigns from the Mission and moves in with her friend Minnie Caldwell.

DECEMBER
★ Ivan and Linda Cheveski decide to emigrate to Canada, where he has found a job as an engineer, and Annie Walker organises a farewell party with drinks and songs round the piano.

1962

JANUARY
★ Ken Barlow angers the neighbourhood when a patronising article criticising the working classes for lack of ambition which he wrote for a left-wing review is reprinted by the *Manchester Evening News* under the heading, 'Life in a Northern Back Street'. Len Fairclough punches him on the jaw in the Rovers.

FEBRUARY
★ Ena makes her peace with Leonard Swindley and returns to live in the vestry.
★ Harry Hewitt exchanges his whippets for a greyhound, Lucky Lolita, and a coach party of friends back it with £10 apiece at Manchester's White City, but it finishes nowhere.

MARCH
★ Ena is found collapsed in the vestry after another stroke.

▼ *The gossip of the Rovers Snug moves to hospital as Minnie Caldwell and Martha Longhurst comfort Ena Sharples after a stroke*

★ Dennis Tanner packs in his job to become a compere at the Orinoco night club, but soon leaves to seek work in London.

APRIL
★ Len Fairclough is sacked from J. Birtwhistle and Sons after being reported by Martha Longhurst for using their materials for private jobs. He buys the yard behind Martha's Mawdesley Street home to start his own building business.

MAY
★ Billy Walker becomes engaged to beauty queen Philippa Scopes but after two weeks they part by mutual consent.
★ Ena Sharples writes to Prince Philip to protest at a council plan to change the name of Coronation Street to Florida Street.
★ Esther Hayes leaves the street and moves into a flat in Moor Lane.

JUNE
★ Christine Hardman suffers a breakdown and threatens suicide on the roof of the raincoat factory, but is talked down to safety by Ken Barlow. Three weeks later she elopes with Colin Appleby.

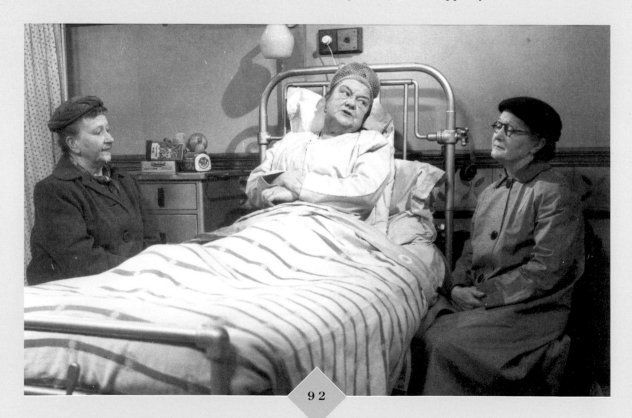

★ Doreen Lostock and Sheila Birtles move into the flat over the corner shop.
★ Bill Gregory, home from sea, takes up with Elsie Tanner again, ignoring Len Fairclough's advice that he should confess he is married.

JULY
★ Bill Gregory's wife arrives at Elsie's home and he leaves to repair his marriage.
★ Ken Barlow becomes engaged to Valerie Tatlock and sells his scooter to pay for the wedding.
★ Len Fairclough recruits an apprentice, Jerry Booth.

AUGUST
★ Ken and Valerie are married, with Lucille as a bridesmaid again, and after a honeymoon in London they move into No 9.
★ Harry and Concepta Hewitt celebrate the arrival of a baby son Christopher, but Lucille is unhappy.
★ Following the death of her mother, Minnie Caldwell moves into No 5, Esther Hayes' old home, with her tabby cat Bobbie.

SEPTEMBER
★ Leonard Swindley enters politics as founder-chairman of the Property Owners and Small Traders Party.
★ Ken Barlow completes his first novel but it is rejected by a publisher.
★ Elsie Tanner begins an association with artful bookie Dave Smith. A jealous Len lashes out at him, is summoned for assault and bound over for a year.

OCTOBER
★ On the Hewitts' first wedding anniversary, baby Christopher is kidnapped from his pram outside Gamma Garments where Lucille had left him unattended. Elsie Tanner traces him and recovers him from a disturbed Joan Akers.
★ Colin Appleby is killed in a car crash; Christine Appleby goes to lodge with Elsie Tanner.
★ Albert Tatlock gets a job as a lollipop man at the crossing near Bessie Street School.

NOVEMBER
★ Christine Appleby takes a job at Miami Modes and begins a friendship with lonely widower Frank Barlow.

▼ *Len Fairclough recruits Jerry Booth as an apprentice after buying a yard and starting his own business*

★ Minnie Caldwell takes in a lodger, Liverpudlian ex-Borstal boy Jed Stone.
★ Leonard Swindley is ignominiously defeated in the local elections, coming bottom of the poll.

DECEMBER
★ Leonard Swindley puts on a production of 'Lady Lawson Loses' at the Mission Hall with Annie Walker in the title role.
★ Len Fairclough's wife Nellie leaves him, taking their 12 year old son Stanley with her, to live with Harry Bailey in Nottingham.
★ Ken Barlow hands in his notice at Bessie Street School to become a full-time writer, then has second thoughts and withdraws it.
★ Bus conductor Johnny Alexander accuses Len Fairclough of fare-dodging and is suspended by Len's friend, bus inspector Harry Hewitt, until Len owns up.

1963

▲ *Shady Jed Stone's market stall is short-lived, as is his relationship with Sheila Birtles*

▶ *Frank Barlow's romance with Christine Appleby is also short-lived. Age difference is the cause*

JANUARY

★ Jed Stone starts a market stall business with Sheila Birtles as his assistant, but her parents forbid her to associate with him.

★ Papagopolous starts a cost-cutting drive at Gamma Garments and instructs Swindley to sack Emily Nugent; Swindley pleads for her and she wins a reprieve provided business picks up.

FEBRUARY

★ Frank Barlow's friendship with much-younger Christine Appleby has tongues wagging and causes a rift with Ken.

MARCH

★ Jed Stone leaves the street in a moonlight flit.

★ Ena Sharples' sister Alice dies at 80, leaving Ena £120, but by the time funeral expenses are paid she is out of pocket.

APRIL

★ The romance between Frank and Christine ends when Christine decides the age gap between them is too great for marriage.

★ Rents go up in Coronation Street and Elsie Tanner is issued with an eviction order after refusing to pay the increase. She concedes only when bailiffs dump her possessions on the pavement.

★ Dennis Tanner returns home to run the Lenny Phillips theatrical agency.

MAY

★ Frank Barlow decides to leave his job with the Post Office and opens a DIY shop in Victoria Street.

★ Elsie Tanner and Len Fairclough go on their first date – dancing at the Orinoco Club.

JUNE

★ Concepta Hewitt's father is ill in Ireland and she persuades Harry to hand in his notice to the busy company and move to live across the sea, but at the last minute he cannot bring himself to leave his teenage daughter Lucille.

JULY

★ Emily Nugent's world is in turmoil as Leonard Swindley is transferred to the head office of Gamma Garments and smooth, womanising Neil Crossley takes over as manager of the Weatherfield shop.

AUGUST

★ Dennis Tanner believes he has made a major talent discovery and launches lanky window cleaner Walter Potts as pop singer Brett Falcon.

★ Albert Tatlock and Alf Roberts have a boozy night out with the Rovers Return darts team and are locked up for assaulting a police officer.

SEPTEMBER

★ Sheila Birtles attempts suicide with an overdose of aspirin when her affair with Neil Crossley ends in tears. Dennis Tanner comes to the rescue, climbing a ladder to the window to wake her from her torpor.

OCTOBER

★ Sheila Birtles abandons her flat over the corner shop and moves in with her parents. Her friend, Doreen Lostock, joins the WRAC.

★ Walter Potts makes a nervous debut at the Weatherfield Trades and Labour Club.

★ Bashful joiner Jerry Booth marries typist Myra Dickinson, and Len Fairclough proposes to Elsie Tanner as his divorce becomes absolute, but she turns him down.

NOVEMBER

★ Elsie launches into an affair with Laurie Frazer, owner of the Orinoco Club.

★ Ena Sharples collapses again and the doctor diagnoses arteriosclerosis; she goes to live with Minnie Caldwell.

DECEMBER

★ Dennis Tanner springs a 'This Is Your Life' on Annie Walker.

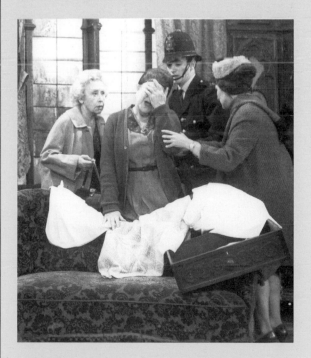

▲ *Ena returns from Jerry and Myra Booth's wedding to find the vestry vandalised*

1964

JANUARY

★ Esther Hayes moves to Glasgow after receiving a Civil Service promotion, and Ken Barlow applies for a higher position at Bessie Street School.

FEBRUARY

★ A Bessie Street School pupil is killed in a road accident nearby and Ken gives an outspoken TV interview which ruins his prospects of promotion at the school.
★ Valerie Barlow leaves Ken for pacifist Dave Robbins, one of his college friends, but returns when Dave declines to take her in.

MARCH

★ Ken becomes head of English at Granston Technical College.
★ Len Fairclough challenges Jerry Booth to a walking race for a £5 wager; fitness fanatic Jerry diplomatically lets his boss win.
★ Laurie Frazer opens the Viaduct Sporting Club in the old raincoat factory.
★ Leonard Swindley, under pressure from Papagopolous, has a nervous breakdown, resigns and moves in with his sister, Hilda Barrett. Florrie Lindley opens a sub post office at the corner shop but also suffers a nervous breakdown and wrecks the place.

APRIL

★ Jerry Booth's wife Myra is pregnant and they are beset with money worries, having fallen behind with mortgage payments.
★ Irma Ogden starts work at the corner shop.

MAY

★ Len Fairclough is forced to sack Jerry because he can no longer afford to employ him; this deepens the Booths' financial difficulties and they move in with Myra's father in Viaduct Street.
★ Frank Barlow has a £5,000 premium bond win and decides to sell his shop and move to Wilmslow. At his celebration party in the Rovers Martha Longhurst dies from a heart attack over a bottle of milk stout in her favourite corner of the Snug.

JUNE

★ Charlie Moffitt, stand-up comic at the Orinoco Club, moves into digs with Minnie Caldwell, accompanied by a greyhound called Little Titch, three pigeons and two rabbits.
★ Dennis Tanner takes up hairdressing and bleaches the hair of Lucille Hewitt, who is already unpopular with her headmistress for having 'Brett Falcon Fan Club' tattooed on her wrist.
★ Stan Ogden pays £200 deposit and takes out a £575 mortgage to buy No 13 Coronation Street.
★ Emily Nugent makes a Leap Year proposal of marriage to Leonard Swindley, whom she has long adored, and he eventually agrees to marry her.

▼ *Time is called for Martha Longhurst, who dies of a stroke in the Rovers Snug*

▶ *Ena Sharples pays her respects to Martha, whose unexpected death robs her of a friend*

JULY

★ The street turns out for the wedding of Swindley and Emily Nugent, but Emily gets an attack of jitters and jilts him at the altar.
★ Elsie Tanner gets a job as a mature model at the School of Design and is flattered by the attention of art teacher David Graham.

AUGUST

★ Graham, infatuated with Elsie, and mentally unbalanced, threatens her with a gun when she tries to end their relationship. Her son Dennis dashes in and overpowers him.
★ Harry and Concepta Hewitt leave for a new life in Castle Blayney in Ireland, where he plans to run a garage.
★ Stan Ogden unearths an unexploded bomb in Albert Tatlock's back garden and the residents of the street are evacuated to the Mission Hall while it is defused.

▼ *Emily Nugent stages the pantomime* Cinderella *at the Mission Hall and fun is had by all*

▶ *Art teacher David Graham threatens Elsie Tanner when she ends their romance*

SEPTEMBER
★ The Ogdens' eldest son, 14 year old Trevor, steals some money and when Irma, his 18 year old sister finds out, he absconds to London.

OCTOBER
★ Minnie Caldwell's Irish lodger, Tickler Murphy, turns wrestling impresario, persuading Stan Ogden to fight formidable Ian Campbell at the Viaduct Sporting Club; Stan is hurled from the ring and counted out sitting in Hilda's lap.
★ Ena Sharples breaks the news to Len Fairclough that Harry Bailey has called to say that Len's ex-wife Nellie is dead.
★ Len proposes to Elsie again, and is again refused, but she agrees to a trial 'daytime marriage'.

NOVEMBER
★ Stan Ogden gets Jack Walker into trouble with the police for selling drinks after hours, when he stops the clock in the Rovers Return.
★ Annie Walker walks out on Jack and the Rovers to stay an a hotel after seeing cheque book stubs he has made out to a Mrs Nicholls. She returns after Billy visits her to explain that Mrs Nicholls is his landlady in London and Jack has been paying Billy's rent on the quiet.

DECEMBER
★ Wealthy butcher William Piggott offers Ken Barlow a £100 bribe to ensure his son passes his school exams; Ken reports him to the police.
★ Footballer David Barlow returns to the street limping and claiming to be out of the game as a result of an injury, but it transpires that he is suspended following allegations that he has taken a bribe. He begins an affair with Irma Ogden.
★ Stan Ogden decides there is a fortune in waste paper and goes into partnership with Albert Tatlock and Charlie Moffitt to collect and sell it.

▼ *Residents are again evacuated to the Mission, when an unexploded bomb is found*

1965

JANUARY

★ Ena Sharples is left No 11 Coronation Street in a will. Tenant Elsie Tanner demands repairs; Ena threatens a rent rise and gives her notice to quit when she complains, but then sells the house to local landlord Edward Wormold for £350.

★ Jerry Booth returns to work for Len Fairclough and becomes Florrie Lindley's lodger after leaving his wife Myra.

FEBRUARY

★ Stan Ogden's waste paper business folds through lack of customers and Stan becomes a milkman.

★ Ena Sharples lends Charlie Moffitt £50 to set up as an insurance agent.

★ Florrie Lindley's engineer husband Norman returns after six years working in the Far East and embarks on an affair with Elsie, inviting her to join him when he starts a new job in Canada.

MARCH

★ Emily Nugent buys a Morris Minor and gets Leonard Swindley to give her driving lessons, but they drive the wrong way up a one-way street, and as his licence has expired both are brought to court. Emily is fined £5 and Swindley £25.

APRIL

★ Ken Barlow becomes the father of twins when Valerie gives birth to Susan and Peter.

★ Brother David Barlow is cleared of soccer bribery allegations but decides to quit league football.

★ William Piggott is fined £150 for trying to bribe Ken. Jerry Booth then obtains a building contract from Piggott, which Len had been expecting to win, and parts from Len to undertake it himself.

MAY

★ Norman and Florrie Lindley are reconciled and she goes with him to Canada after selling the corner shop to Lionel Petty.

★ David Barlow signs a two-year contract as player-coach of Weatherfield Athletic football club.

▲ *Stan Ogden, Dennis Tanner and Jed Stone together – it can only mean trouble*

JUNE

★ Lionel Petty's daughter Sandra serves in the corner shop and falls for her first customer, Dennis Tanner.

★ David Barlow and Irma Ogden decide to get engaged on a trip to the Blue John mines at Speedwell in Derbyshire.

★ Ena Sharples accepts an invitation to visit relatives in Nebraska and flies out while Clare Midgeley stands in for her at the Mission.

JULY

★ Elsie Tanner, recruited by Emily Nugent to work at Gamma Garments in March, is sacked by Emily in a staff economy drive, and takes a job at the local launderette.

★ Stan Ogden and Charlie Moffitt brew their own beer at Minnie Caldwell's house – until bottles begin to explode and Minnie declares prohibition.

▲ *New corner shop owner Lionel Petty's daughter falls for Dennis Tanner, pictured with Lucille Hewitt*

◄ *Stan Ogden and Charlie Moffitt provide the refreshments on a trip to Derbyshire*

► *Elsie Tanner is picked up in a pub by Robert Maxwell, who then dies at the wheel of his Jaguar, but she manages to escape unhurt. His widow blames Elsie, but a coroner concludes it was death from natural causes*

AUGUST

★ Jerry Booth's solo business venture for Piggott fails and he is forced to return cap in hand to Len, who offers him a partnership. Their first job is demolishing No 7, which collapsed after Harry and Concepta Hewitt left for Ireland.

★ Teenage rebel Lucille Hewitt surprises with her exam results – four O levels including science and geography.

SEPTEMBER

★ Elsie is picked up by tweedy Robert Maxwell in a Cheshire pub but he collapses and dies behind the wheel of his Jaguar. The coroner's verdict is death from natural causes but Maxwell's widow blames Elsie.

OCTOBER

★ Coronation Street's ladies take part in a charity mannequin parade at the Mission Hall organised by Emily Nugent.

★ Lucille quits her job in a mail order firm and goes to work in research and development at Marshall's cotton mill.

NOVEMBER

★ Annie Walker is installed as chairman of the Lady Victuallers and invested with a chain of office.

★ Dennis Tanner has a phone installed at No 11 and Elsie has a whirlwind affair with the telephone engineer, Jim Mount.

▼ *David Barlow and Irma Ogden get an unexpected reception at their planned low-key wedding*

DECEMBER

★ David Barlow and Irma Ogden decide to marry in secret at a register office but a cabbie blabs and the entire street arrives for their reception at the Greenvale Hotel.

★ Lucille is caught serving behind the bar of the Rovers while under age by Jack Turner who tries to blackmail Jack Walker until Jerry Booth sorts him out.

★ David Barlow suffers a leg injury in a charity football match and is told he will not play soccer again. His contract is terminated with £300 compensation.

1966

JANUARY

★ Val Barlow is given a piano and takes lessons from Ena Sharples, while Ken falls for *Weatherfield Gazette* reporter Jackie Marsh, who wrote about David's accident.

★ David and Irma Barlow decide to buy the corner shop from Lionel Petty.

★ Stan Ogden thinks he has won a fortune on the football pools – until he finds Hilda has filled in the coupon incorrectly.

★ Minnie Caldwell celebrates the surprise return of her lodger Jed Stone after an unexplained absence.

FEBRUARY

★ Emily Nugent, offered a job managing a souvenir shop in Majorca, is given a farewell party, but instead of flying to Majorca goes to Harrogate to nurse her father who has suffered a stroke.

★ Albert Tatlock and Clara Midgeley go on holiday to Cleveleys together.

★ Ray Langton, a plumber hired by Jerry Booth in Len's absence, plunges into an affair with Lucille. When they baby-sit for the Barlows he steals £5.

MARCH

★ Clara Midgeley tries to snare Albert Tatlock into marriage but when she rearranges his furniture for the first time in 20 years he decides she is too pushy.

★ Elsie cuts off her connection with phone engineer Jim Mount when she realises he has no intention of marrying her. He leaves the street with Brenda Riley, who has been standing in at the Rovers while Annie is on holiday.

★ Jed Stone and Dennis Tanner go into business with a boarding kennel under the Viaduct.

APRIL

★ Valerie discovers Ken's romance with Jackie Marsh but he claims it was merely a platonic friendship.

★ Ray Langton is sacked by Len Fairclough after stealing a bottle of whisky from the Rovers and threatening Lucille with violence if she talks. He leaves the street.

★ Ena Sharples, who has given her life savings to her hard-up daughter Vera, is

▼ *Hilda Ogden and daughter Irma are unaware of cattle surrounding their caravan on a Welsh holiday*

fined £2 for shoplifting from a supermarket. The Mission is again scheduled for demolition and social worker Ruth Winter tries to rehouse her but Ena refuses to move.

MAY

★ Lucille and Irma take £15-a-week jobs at the newly-opened Elliston's raincoat factory. Another worker there is Bet Lynch, whom Annie Walker describes as 'rather common'.

★ Stan Ogden begins selling ice cream after his morning milk round but is unable to lick the established Italian Bonartis who take all his custom.

JUNE

★ The Bonartis offer Stan an ice cream round but Hilda suspects him of an affair with Mrs Rose Bonarti and reports him for trading without a licence.

★ Sheila Birtles returns from Rawtenstall to work in the raincoat factory, moves in with Elsie and resumes her affair with Jerry Booth.

JULY

★ Dennis Tanner runs up a £94 gambling debt which bookmaker Dave Smith offers to forget in return for favours from Elsie, but she declines and Len Fairclough gives Dennis a job to bail him out of trouble.

★ Ken Barlow arranges an evening of cultural films at the Mission Hall but the distributors send him nudist films by mistake.

AUGUST

★ Jerry seeks a divorce from Myra but meets fierce opposition from her father, George Dickinson.

SEPTEMBER

★ Len Fairclough opposes Annie Walker in the local council elections and the result is a tie, even after a recount. Eventually Len wins on the toss of a coin.

★ Jed Stone is arrested at Minnie's birthday party and is sentenced to 18 months in prison for receiving stolen blankets.

OCTOBER

★ Ivan and Linda Cheveski return from Canada and Elsie Tanner is sacked from the launderette for taking time off. Elsie also gets anonymous phone calls, which are traced to the widow of Robert Maxwell, who has become mentally disturbed.

★ Jed Stone sends word from Liverpool's Walton jail to Minnie asking her to auction his belongings. Annie Walker buys a two-bob cameo brooch which she later finds to be worth £15.

NOVEMBER

★ Young Paul Cheveski is pulled from the canal by an unknown rescuer. Elsie rounds on Len who blocked council proposals to fence the canal for financial reasons, and Ivan gets into a punch-up with Len.

DECEMBER

★ Stan is made redundant from his milk round and faces Christmas on the dole.

★ Elsie returns to Miami Modes as supervisor.

★ Ex-Gamma Garments manager Neil Crossley leaves the street with Sheila Birtles; they plan to marry.

★ Ena's daughter Vera is unwell and Ena accuses her of malingering, not knowing Vera is dying of a brain tumour.

★ Val and Ken Barlow celebrate Christmas by throwing a fancy dress party at the Mission, at which Annie Walker appears as Elizabeth I.

▲ *The disturbed widow of Robert Maxwell confronts Elsie Tanner with more than a sharp tongue*

◀ *Annie Walker takes advantage of the Mission's fancy-dress party to take off Elizabeth I*

1967

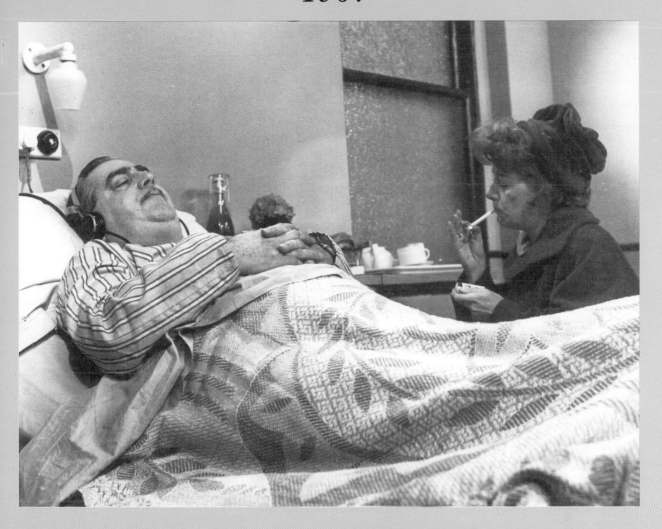

▲ *A sprained back gives Stan Ogden the lifestyle to which he is accustomed. Hilda keeps an eye on him*

JANUARY
★ Stan Ogden's dole money is stopped when he refuses work, and he takes a job as a coal heaver.
★ Dennis Tanner leaves the yard after setting fire to Len's kitchen with a blow torch while decorating it. Emily Nugent gives him a job at Gamma Garments and he persuades Lucille to join him.
★ Percy Bridge poses as the man who rescued Paul Cheveski from the canal and accepts a reward from Elsie, but is exposed by Dave Smith who was the real rescuer.
★ Ena's daughter Vera dies from a brain tumour.

FEBRUARY
★ Stan Ogden takes over Dennis Tanner's job at Len's yard and enjoys a week on sick pay after spraining his back.
★ Albert Tatlock is knocked unconscious during a raid on Dave Smith's betting shop while placing a bet for Minnie Caldwell, and Ena launches a petition to get the shop closed down.

MARCH
★ Ken is arrested on a student demo against the war in Vietnam, refuses to pay a £5 fine and opts for seven days' imprisonment.

APRIL
★ Minnie Caldwell receives £50 from a 30 year old insurance policy but a conman posing as a plumber relieves her of £20 of it.

◄After giving up professional football through injury, David Barlow coaches a women's soccer team, the Weatherfield Hotspurs

★ David Barlow becomes coach to the Weatherfield Hotspurs all-ladies soccer team.

MAY

★ Elsie Tanner's wartime sweetheart Master Sgt Steve Tanner of the US army is posted to Burtonwood and she and Steve rekindle their love affair.

★ A goods train ploughs through the viaduct parapet and plunges into the street. Sonia Peters, a former schoolfriend of Lucille's, is killed; her boyfriend, PC Jimmy Conway, is dragged from the rubble by Jerry Booth. Ena Sharples is feared dead, but is dug out of the wreckage by David Barlow.

JUNE

★ Steve Tanner is roughed up by Dot Greenhalgh's husband, Walter, who thinks he is Greg Flint, his wife's American friend. On a night out at an inn in Cheshire Steve proposes to Elsie and she accepts.

★ Dennis Tanner's blonde Swedish girlfriend Inga Olsen goes to Amsterdam and he follows her.

JULY

★ Squatters Betty Lawson and her sons Clifford and Ronnie take over No 3. Val Barlow sympathises with them but Ken demands Len Fairclough has them evicted.

★ Lucille sends for a cosmetics brochure in Annie Walker's name as a joke, but Annie laughs last when she wins a weekend in Paris with a film star as the company's millionth customer.

★ Dennis Tanner turns up with his latest girlfriend, Karen, sister of Inga. He tries to register her as his au pair and, when visited by a consular official, borrows Val's twins and talks Lucille into posing as his wife, but the official is not fooled.

AUGUST

★ Hilda is seen boarding a Liverpool-bound bus in her slippers and police find her wandering in a disturbed state near the pierhead. In her purse she has £40 which Stan was holding as treasurer of the Rovers Outing Fund. The money is refunded but Stan loses it to Albert Tatlock at cards.

★ Steve Tanner and Len challenge Albert to a game of pitch and toss to get the money back but he wins again. Then, satisfied that he has taught Stan a lesson, Albert gives the cash back.

★ Emily organises a coach trip to Tatton Park.

SEPTEMBER

★ Steve and Elsie marry and leave for a honeymoon in Lisbon, but the day is marred when Harry Hewitt, over from Ireland for the wedding, is crushed to death when a jack collapses under Len's van after a breakdown on the way to the reception.

★ With Elsie away on honeymoon, Dennis Tanner takes in theatrical lodgers ranging from a couple of acrobats and their mother to a girls' pipe band.

▲ *Jerry Booth and David Barlow fear for Ena when a train ploughs through the viaduct*

▼ *A honeymoon in Lisbon gives a happy start to Steve and Elsie Tanner's doomed marriage*

OCTOBER

★ Len Fairclough's problem son Stanley comes to live with him and there is friction immediately. Stanley sets fire to Len's yard, is overcome by the heat and smoke, and Len collapses as he tries to drag him clear. Stan Ogden rescues him and Stanley returns to stepfather Harry Bailey.

★ Emily Nugent visits a marriage bureau and her first date – on her 38th birthday – is with farmer Frank Starkey, but she is terrified by the cows on his farm.

NOVEMBER

★ Elsie Tanner's American mother-in-law Emmeline arrives to meet her new daughter-in-law, disapproves and there is a row.

★ Emily Nugent has another marriage bureau date and becomes engaged to hotelier Douglas Preston, but backs off when she realises he is only motivated by the thought of escape from his sister's domination.

DECEMBER

★ Annie Walker, visiting a football match for the first time, is harrassed by hooligans, throws a rattle at them and breaks a window by mistake. She is arrested but Len Fairclough gets charges dropped.

★ Irma Barlow, after a miscarriage, tries to adopt a baby but is turned down. She and David foster Jilly Morris for Christmas.

★ When Elsie and Steve leave for America, Dennis Tanner turns No 11 into a hippy commune.

1968

JANUARY

★ Ena is evicted from the Mission as bull-dozers move in to demolish her home of 30 years, along with the raincoat factory. She leaves for St Anne's to be housekeeper to Henry Foster, a wealthy friend of her late husband.

★ Irma Barlow fixes a date for lonely Emily with macho Hungarian building worker Miklos Zadic.

★ Hilda, neglected by Stan, strikes up a relationship with park gardener George Greenwood, who buys her a budgie which he keeps in his hut, but they part when Stan finds out.

★ Lucille joins the hippy commune at No 11.

★ Dennis Tanner gets himself a new girl-friend, cockney Jenny Sutton, sister of one of the hippies, and they join the staff of Weatherfield Social Club as waiter and re-ceptionist.

FEBRUARY

★ Elsie returns alone from America after Steve is posted to Panama. Their marriage appears to be over.

★ Annie Walker is kidnapped and held for £5 ransom by rag students. When nobody offers to pay the ransom, a miffed Annie is obliged to pay it herself.

▼ *Emily Nugent finds short-lived happiness with Hungarian building worker Miklos Zadic*

MARCH

★ Dennis returns from London with girl-friend Jenny and becomes a rep for Crowning Glory hairdressing requisites.

APRIL

★ David and Irma Barlow, who is pregnant, emigrate to Australia, selling the corner shop to Les and Maggie Clegg.

★ Miklos takes a job in Newcastle and Emily leaves with him but three weeks later she is back, tight-lipped about what went wrong, and lodges at the Rovers.

▶ *It's students' Rag Week and Annie Walker is kidnapped for a £5 ransom, which she pays herself when no one else shows the inclination*

MAY

★ When Len Fairclough advertises for a plumber, Jerry Booth recruits Ray Langton in Len's absence. Len is furious and he and Ray come to blows.

★ Dennis borrows £100 from a loan shark at 48 per cent interest to marry Jenny Sutton. On his wedding night his boss orders him to Bristol immediately, and he leaves Jenny alone in a double bed.

JUNE

★ After being allocated one of the street's new maisonettes built by Len, Ken Barlow sells his Mini to buy furniture for it. Ena also returns to occupy a maisonette.

★ Dickie Fleming, aged 19, and Audrey Bright, 17, buy Frank Barlow's old home, No 3, for £400, and Len Fairclough buys No 9 for £1,000.

★ Les Clegg is admitted to a mental hospital suffering from alcoholism and Ena lends a hand at the corner shop.

JULY

★ Ena's new neighbour is Jack Walker's childhood sweetheart, Effie Spicer, but Annie Walker warns her off when she joins Jack's bowling club and calls him by his pet name, 'Jonty'.

★ Ray Langton becomes Elsie's lodger and makes overtures to her, whereupon she evicts him and Len takes him in at No 9.

★ Dickie Fleming and Audrey Bright elope to Gretna to marry.

★ Papagopolous goes bankrupt and Emily Nugent and Lucille are out of work.

AUGUST

★ Valerie Barlow is held prisoner in her maisonette by escaped convict Frank Riley while Ken is attending a drama class, but she manages to tap out a signal on the central heating pipes and Ena raises the alarm.

★ Dave Smith buys the old Gamma Garments shop and opens it as a flower shop, the Pink Posy, with Elsie Tanner as manageress.

SEPTEMBER

★ Steve Tanner persuades two army pals to set up a meeting with Elsie but she refuses to go to America with him. Shortly afterwards Steve is found dead at the foot of stairs to his flat.

★ Emily Nugent agrees to look after Tommy Deakin's donkey Dolores while he is away and gets Maggie Clegg to keep it behind the shop, but so many customers complain about the smell Annie is obliged to let her use the pub yard.

★ Audrey Fleming, who has become a filling station attendant at the Blue Bell garage, wins £50 as Miss Petrol Pump.

OCTOBER

★ Detectives investigating Steve Tanner's death question Len Fairclough, who has an injured hand, while Elsie goes on holiday with bookie Dave Smith.

NOVEMBER

★ Gordon Clegg, trainee accountant son of Les and Maggie, wants to marry Lucille Hewitt but his mother will not allow it.

★ Ken takes up the trumpet again and plays at the Ogdens' wedding anniversary.

DECEMBER

★ Lucille and Gordon, set on getting married, run off to Gretna Green but get cold feet in the buffet at Preston station and return home sheepishly.

★ Albert Tatlock, who has been in Bury as curator of his old regimental museum, returns to live at No 1.

★ Rovers regulars stage the Christmas panto *Aladdin* with Emily Nugent and the vicar, the Rev Reginald James, producing.

★ Marjorie Griffin, an old flame of Len's, turns up on his doorstep having left her husband, and moves in with him.

▲ *Stan and Hilda Ogden show themselves to be cut out for pantomime, appearing in Aladdin*

1969

JANUARY
★ Billy Walker returns from London with Chinese girlfriend Jasmine Chong, but she declines to marry him and goes back to London.
★ Len Fairclough tries to scare off Marjorie by proposing to her, but she accepts. Her ex-husband Basil calls to dump her clothes and pet monkey Marlon. Len bribes two children to pose as his sons, and Marjorie finally goes.

FEBRUARY
★ Ray Langton's deliquent sister, Janice, who is on probation, arrives at No 9; Len likes her and lets her stay.
★ Minnie Caldwell, who has been gambling secretly and owes Dave Smith £10, disappears, leaving a note saying, 'Look after the cat,' and is taken to hospital after collapsing in the street.
★ Janice and her boyfriend Bob Neale disappear in Dave Smith's Jaguar. Ena blackmails him into wiping out Minnie's debt by threatening to tell the Inland Revenue about his expensive car.
★ Gordon Clegg passes his accountancy exam and buys Lucille an engagement ring.

MARCH
★ Lucille Hewitt goes ahead with wedding plans and buys a dress but Gordon backs out at the last minute, and they part as friends.
★ Pensioner Alice Pickens becomes Albert Tatlock's lodger, determined to become his bride later.

APRIL
★ Albert Tatlock pitches Alice out, along with her mynah bird Kitchener, stacking her belongings on the pavement. She is forced to move in with Minnie.
★ Dave Smith's wife Lillian hires a private eye to tail Elsie Tanner with the threat of divorce proceedings until he agrees to pay her a weekly allowance.
★ Ena is arrested after organising a sit-in against plans to demolish the pensioners' club room.
★ Ray Langton begins an affair with newly-wed Audrey Fleming.

MAY
★ Alice Pickens packs her bags and leaves to look after an elderly uncle in West Hartlepool.
★ Annie Walker canvasses for signatures for a Perfect Landlady competition she has entered and wins a holiday for two in Majorca, but instead of taking Jack she takes Ena Sharples.

JUNE
★ Maggie Clegg's sister Betty Turpin arrives with her police sergeant husband Cyril. As no police house is available they stay at the corner shop and Betty becomes a barmaid at the Rovers.
★ Unknown to Len, it is Elsie who bails him out of financial trouble with a loan made through Jack Walker. Len then confesses he needed the money to marry town hall clerk Janet Reid. And when she turns him down, he blames Elsie and slaps her. She leaves in a taxi vowing never to return.
★ Emily meets photographer Ernest Bishop at his mother's funeral and accepts an offer to work in his shop.

◀ *Hilda Ogden takes to crystal ball-gazing and is soon giving the locals her view of their future*

▲ *New Rovers barmaid Betty Turpin and policeman husband Cyril stay with her sister Maggie Clegg*

JULY
★ Len traces Elsie to Scarborough and sells his van to repay her loan.
★ Stan Ogden borrows £50 to buy 50 suit lengths in the market, reckoning he can get a tenner for each. But Hilda, believing them stolen, sells them for £1 each.
★ When Alice Pickens appears at Albert Tatlock's regimental museum while he is conducting a tour he falls off the platform in shock, suffering a broken arm and two cracked ribs.

AUGUST
★ Ray Langton engages Audrey Fleming as a clerk.
★ Egged on by Val and Ken, Albert proposes to Alice and she books a honeymoon suite in Morecambe. On his stag night he is found wrapped around a lamp post singing 'If I Ruled the World'.

SEPTEMBER
★ Albert and Alice get to the church on time but the vicar does not. His car breaks down, and Albert and Alice call off the marriage. Rather than waste the tickets Albert goes to Morecambe alone on holiday.
★ Stan Ogden takes up primitive sculpting and sets up an exhibition in Bernard Fleming's gallery but the dustmen think his exhibits are junk and cart them away.

OCTOBER
★ Squatters move into the empty flat next to Ken and Val, and Ken supports their cause when he finds out their spokesman is his old college friend Dave Robbins, but Val wants them out.
★ At Miami Modes Elsie collects a parcel for Dot Greenhalgh, is stopped by security men and finds it contains stolen dresses. She is charged with theft and although the case is dismissed for lack of evidence she loses her job.

NOVEMBER
★ On a Rovers outing to Windermere the hired coach has faulty steering and runs off a moorland road. The driver dies and all the passengers are injured, most seriously Minnie Caldwell who is unconscious and Ray Langton who is paralysed from the waist down.

DECEMBER
★ Alan Howard, who served in the Royal Navy with Len Fairclough, borrows Len's house while he is away. Alan plans to open a hairdressing salon at the Pink Posy and offers Valerie Barlow the job of manageress.
★ Ray Langton leaves hospital in a wheelchair and goes to stay with Dickie and Audrey Fleming.
★ At a Christmas talent night Ken Barlow plays trumpet, Albert recites a monologue, Irma Barlow, visiting on holiday, impersonates Hylda Baker, and Minnie Caldwell recites 'The Owl and the Pussycat'.

1970

JANUARY

★ Elsie Tanner and Alan Howard start a 'no strings' relationship.

★ Maggie Clegg sues her husband Les for divorce and Len has a brief fling with her, before moving on to take up with a barmaid at the Flying Horse.

FEBRUARY

★ Bill Gregory, now retired from the sea and a widower, proposes to Elsie that she marries him and joins him in his new business in Portugal. She turns him down, realising she is in love with Alan.

★ Emily Nugent accepts a partnership in Ernest Bishop's photographic business.

MARCH

★ Annie Walker stages a Lysistrata-style protest, persuading the girls to withhold all favours from their men until the men sign a petition protesting against the football match bus stopping in Coronation Street.

APRIL

★ Hilda hears that David Barlow and her grandson Darren have been killed in a car crash in Australia, and Dave Smith lends her £600 to fly out and bring Irma home.

MAY

★ *Weatherfield Gazette* readers raise £600 for Hilda to repay Dave, but Stan uses the money to buy Irma a partnership in the corner shop.

★ Dickie and Audrey Fleming part company after her affair with Ray Langton.

★ Police Sgt Turpin comes home to find Betty terrorised by Keith Lucas, whom he once put in prison. He relieves Lucas of an iron bar in a struggle and is only prevented from killing Lucas by Len.

JUNE

★ After a disciplinary hearing, Cyril is obliged to retire from the force and takes a clerical job which provides a house into which he and Betty move.

★ Jack Walker dies suddenly on a visit to his daughter Joan and is buried near her home in Derby.

JULY

★ Under the strain of widowhood, Irma Barlow snatches a baby, but Emily Nugent and Bet Lynch manage to return the child before the police are called.

★ Alan Howard and Elsie Tanner are married quietly and leave for a Paris honeymoon.

▶ *Having ditched old flame Bill Gregory, Elsie Tanner and Alan Howard have a quiet register office wedding, after informal drinks at the Rovers. Then, it's a honeymoon in romantic Paris*

▶ *Len Fairclough, watched by Maggie Clegg, has his eye on Bet Lynch, who gives up her job at the launderette to become a barmaid at the Rovers Return*

When they return, a cheque Alan has given to Ray bounces.

AUGUST
★ Alan Howard is close to bankruptcy. He has sold the hairdressing salon and Billy Walker, home after his father's death, offers him a mechanic's job in the new garage he is opening in Canal Street.
★ Ena discovers a boy prodigy organist, Tony Parsons, and is determined to get him into a college of music.

SEPTEMBER
★ Elsie Tanner takes a job as a rep with Charm Cosmetics.
★ Bet Lynch takes up with ex-Borstal boy Frank Bradley and it emerges that she has an illegitimate son.
★ Maggie Clegg and Irma go on holiday leaving Hilda Ogden in charge of the shop; she stocks up with fancy foods no one wants to buy.

OCTOBER
★ By the time Irma gets back to the shop her mother has made a large loss and half the customers have taken their custom elsewhere.

NOVEMBER
★ Albert finds out that Handel Gartside, Minnie's old school friend, was a conscien-

▼ *Shortly before Jack Walker's untimely death, Stan Ogden enjoys his hospitality*

tious objector in World War One, and sends him a white feather.
★ A mystery is solved when Joe Donnelli, an American army deserter, takes lodgings at Minnie's and, holding Irma prisoner, confesses that he killed Steve Tanner by striking his head against a wall and throwing him down stairs, because Steve had been pressing him for repayment of a debt.

DECEMBER
★ Irma escapes from Joe Donnelli but he holds Minnie at gunpoint. Stan goes to her rescue and Donnelli turns the gun and kills himself.
★ Bet Lynch quits her job at the launderette to become a barmaid at the Rovers.

1971

JANUARY
★ Ken Barlow accepts a teaching post in Montego Bay and he and Val prepare for a new future, but on the night of his farewell celebration Valerie is electrocuted by a faulty hair dryer plug.

FEBRUARY
★ After Val's funeral the twins go to relatives in Glasgow while Ken moves into the Bay Tree Hotel where he is comforted by receptionist Yvonne Chapel.
★ The flats where Val died are demolished because of structural faults, and a new community centre and warehouse are planned for the site.
★ Billy Walker takes Alan, Elsie and Irma on a joyride in Weatherfield's mayoral Rolls-Royce, but on the return journey hits a Mini outside a chip shop.

MARCH
★ Emily Nugent tries to organise a protest demo against the new warehouse but gets little support; when she forms a human barricade herself she is covered in sand from a dump truck.
★ Ken Barlow takes on housekeeper Margaret Lacey to look after the twins but she resigns after Lucille Hewitt recognises her as a nurse who ill-treated her when she was in an orphanage.

APRIL
★ Annie Walker goes on a Greek cruise ship holiday with local butcher Arthur Dewhurst, but Billy sees him as a rogue.
★ Ray and Irma find Stan Ogden sleeping on the job as a nightwatchman at Hulme's bakery and take his van into town as a joke. When Stan is sacked, Ray gives him a job to compensate.

MAY
★ Elsie gets a job as supervisor at the warehouse.
★ Ena Sharples scares off new community centre caretaker Hetty Thorpe with tales of hooliganism – then takes over herself.

JUNE
★ Stan Ogden is convinced he is being exploited and forms his own trade union, the Stanley Ogden District Union (SODU for short). But when Len finds Stan is being paid £1 over the union rate he cuts his pay.

JULY
★ Ernest Bishop and Emily have a tiff but make it up and become engaged.
★ Billy Walker moves to a self-service petrol station in Chiswick and hands over the garage to Alan Howard to manage.

AUGUST
★ Ernest Bishop loses Emily's £100 engagement ring and Stan Ogden is suspected of stealing it until it is found in Ernest's trouser turn-up.
★ Former town hall clerk Janet Reid, now working at the corner shop, makes a secret date with Alan Howard in Leeds but Elsie finds out.

▲ *Alan Howard fails to keep a secret date with Janet Reid from wife Elsie*

SEPTEMBER
★ Ernest Bishop goes on a photographic assignment to Spain.
★ Hilda Ogden, determined to keep up with the Joneses, badgers Stan into making a serving hatch between their kitchen and living room and throws a party to show it off, but only Ena turns up.

OCTOBER
★ Ken Barlow proposes to hotel receptionist Yvonne Chapel but she feels unable to cope with the twins.
★ Jerry Booth returns jobless and moves in with Len and Ray, then thumps a customer unconscious in the Rovers and receives a 12 month conditional discharge.
★ Ernest Bishop, photographing a scantily clad model in Spain, is charged with offending public morality.

NOVEMBER
★ Emily flies to Spain to plead for Ernest while Annie Walker petitions the Spanish embassy.
★ Lucille becomes a go-go dancer at the Aquarius Club.

▲ *A flower show brings colour to the lives of Minnie Caldwell, Ena Sharples and Albert Tatlock*

▼ *Physiotherapist Lorna Shorecross lodges with Annie Walker and catches son Billy's eye*

DECEMBER
★ Footballer Eddie Duncan transfers his attentions from Irma Barlow to Bet Lynch.
★ A £500 premium bond windfall pays off Hilda's debt to Dave Smith.

1972

JANUARY
★ Ken Barlow is appointed deputy head at Bessie Street School.
★ Footballer Eddie Duncan is transferred to Torquay United. He leaves without Bet Lynch but Irma Barlow follows him.
★ Billy Walker sells his share in the garage for £2,500.

FEBRUARY
★ Stan Ogden promises Hilda a birthday trip to Paris but they miss the plane, spend the day at the airport, and pretend to the neighbours that they have been abroad.
★ Ken strikes up a friendship with Rita Bates, mother of one of his pupils.
★ Alfred Tatlock is appointed assistant caretaker at the community centre after a break-in and theft of a colour TV set.
★ Cyril and Betty Turpin offer to buy Irma's share in the corner shop from Maggie Clegg but she turns them down, and Gordon lends her the money to buy it herself.

MARCH
★ Jerry Booth constructs an 11 ft sailing dinghy, the *Shangri-La*, in Len's yard but on its maiden voyage, with Ray Langton and Stan Ogden as crew, it capsizes.

APRIL
★ Ernest Bishop and Emily Nugent are married on Easter Monday in the Mawdesley Street Congregational Church and set up home at No 3, while Ken moves into No 1 with Albert Tatlock.

MAY
★ Ken becomes more involved with Rita Bates and gets a warning to stop from his headmaster. Len takes up with her instead and finds out she is not married to Harry Bates but merely living with him. Nor is she the mother of his children.
★ Stan Ogden becomes a long-distance lorry driver but on his first run, delivering bananas to Newcastle, he crashes while trying to avoid a fox.
★ While Stan is away, Hilda's brother Archie Crabtree delights her by building a porch over her front door, but then has to

▼ *Stan and Hilda miss the plane for her birthday trip to Paris*

remove it because he has not obtained planning permission.

JUNE
★ An endowment policy of Elsie's matures and she has a pink bathroom suite installed at No 11.
★ Maggie Clegg gets a new shop assistant – Norma Ford – whose father, Jackie, emerging from prison, is invited to stay.
★ Len resumes his affair with Rita, who is singing at the New Victoria Working Men's Club under her real name, Rita Littlewood, Harry Bates having gone back to his wife.

JULY
★ Benny Lewis opens a new betting shop in Dave Smith's old premises, and Emily and Ena ask him to limit Minnie's betting.
★ Alan Howard's ex-wife Laura calls, offering to wipe off the sum he borrowed to buy the garage, but Elsie says they will repay in full.

◄ *Having previously jilted Leonard Swindley, Emily Nugent makes it to the altar for Ernest Bishop*

▲ *Rita Littlewood turns heads while singing at the newly opened Capricorn nightclub*

AUGUST
★ Rita Littlewood accepts a proposal of marriage from Benny Lewis, then rejects him in favour of Len Fairclough.
★ Maggie Clegg meets draughtsman Ron Cooke through a lonely hearts ad placed without her knowledge by Norma Ford, but stops seeing him when she discovers he has an alcoholic past.
★ A peeping-tom is at large and his victims include Lucille, Hilda, Emily and Elsie.

SEPTEMBER
★ Ena is on a street outing to Preston when her grandson Colin Lomax and his wife Karen visit the street from West Hartlepool; their baby son Jason is kidnapped from outside the Rovers but is found again by Emily Bishop and Betty Turpin.
★ Alf Roberts' wife Phyllis dies in hospital.
★ Annie Walker is rushed to hospital when Lucille suspects she has taken a drug overdose.

OCTOBER
★ Stan Ogden beats Piggy Owen from the Flying Horse to win the beer drinking contest in the Weatherfield Pub Olympics.
★ Concepta Hewitt arrives from Ireland with fiancé Sean Regan to visit Lucille.

NOVEMBER
★ Concepta returns to Ireland, unaware that Sean has made a pass at Bet Lynch.
★ Rita sings at the newly opened night club, the Capricorn, financed by Alan Howard, Jimmy Frazer and Benny Lewis.

DECEMBER
★ Hilda now has three cleaning jobs – at the Rovers, the betting shop and the Capricorn, and Stan thinks it is time he retired.
★ Len Fairclough and Alf Roberts are both running to be next mayor of Weatherfield.
★ The whole street takes part in Ernest and Emily Bishop's Christmas Day 1940s Show, with Annie Walker as Britannia.

1973

JANUARY

★ Widower Alf Roberts is named mayor-elect and asks Maggie to become his Mayoress. When she refuses, Annie Walker accepts and takes elocution lessons.

★ Alan and Elsie Howard row over his drink problem, but make it up and plan a fresh start. Lucille Hewitt, fed up with being bossed by Annie Walker, moves in with them.

FEBRUARY

★ Hilda celebrates her 49th birthday with a Barbara Cartland party. Billy Walker is caught in Stan's bedroom with Edna Gee and is mistaken for Ernest Bishop who is too drunk for explanations.

★ Alf Roberts knocks down an elderly woman while giving a late-night lift to Bet Lynch. The victim's son tries to blackmail Alf for £200 but Bet gets his cheque back.

MARCH

★ Jerry Booth causes a gas leak when he replaces Albert Tatlock's old gas cooker with a new electric one, and Albert is hospitalised while neighbours are evacuated to the community centre.

▲ Only Hilda Ogden would think of staging a Barbara Cartland-style party for a birthday celebration, and the drink flows

APRIL

★ Emily is jealous when Ernest asks Rita to tout for photographic jobs on a commission basis and tries to outshine her by taking pictures of strippers at a local club.

★ Stan and Hilda have a mouse in the house and Elsie Tanner tips off the public health inspector who has the house fumigated.

MAY

★ Alf Roberts and Annie Walker become mayor and mayoress of Weatherfield, but caterers refuse to supply food for the celebration party when Billy Walker's cheque bounces; he has been gambling with the pub funds.

★ Len Fairclough buys a shop in Rosamund Street, names it the Kabin and puts Rita in as manageress.

★ There is a street outing to Woburn Abbey where Minnie buys a souvenir tea towel from the Duke of Bedford.

JUNE

★ Rita enlists Mavis Riley as her assistant in the Kabin.

★ The street pools syndicate wins first dividend on the pools but Stan Ogden has forgotten to pass on Bet, Elsie and Alan Howard's stake money to Ray, who refuses to share the winnings.

JULY

★ Ray relents over the £300 pools win and gives Bet, Alan and Elsie £75 each, but the Ogdens get nothing.

★ Telling Alan she is visiting Sheila Crossley in Sheffield, Elsie goes secretly to London to see Dennis who is in Pentonville Prison for swindling pensioners in a double glazing racket. Knocked down by a taxi she lies in hospital, unidentified, suffering from concussion.

AUGUST

★ Elsie is identified by the police and Alan goes to visit her.

SEPTEMBER

★ Ray recruits Deirdre Hunt to work in the yard.

★ Ken Barlow begins an affair with Janet Reid.

OCTOBER

★ Ken brings the twins from Glasgow to meet Janet. They marry at her parents' home in Keswick.

★ Ena, under threat of dismissal from the community centre, suffers a heart attack in the Snug.

NOVEMBER

★ Ken and Janet quarrel over the choice of a house; he refuses to look at one priced at £11,500 and misses out on another.

DECEMBER

★ Albert proposes to Minnie for financial reasons. She accepts but is relieved when he has second thoughts.

★ Ena is sacked from the community centre for inefficiency. Minnie accuses the Bishops of victimising her and they are sent to Coventry by the street. On New Year's eve Ena moves to St Anne's on Sea.

★ Len and Rita announce their marriage.

★ Stan and Hilda have a reunion with their ne'er do well son Trevor, who is living in Chesterfield, and are surprised to discover they are grandparents; Trevor had told his wife his parents were dead.

◄ *When Alf Roberts becomes Mayor of Weatherfield, Annie Walker gladly agrees to be Mayoress*

▼ *The Duke of Bedford is present on a street residents' trip to Woburn Abbey*

1974

JANUARY
★ Len tells Rita that a property company has plans to demolish the street and redevelop it, and Rita lets it slip in the Rovers.
★ Billy Walker returns and agrees to buy the garage from Alan Howard.

FEBRUARY
★ When Len refuses to attend a protest meeting about the development he is sent to Coventry and a brick is hurled through his window by Emily Bishop. In fact, Len has voted against the plan, causing its defeat.
★ Cyril Turpin collapses and dies and Betty becomes confused.

MARCH
★ Betty Turpin finds her late husband Cyril left only £859 and moves in with her sister Maggie, hoping to sell the house.
★ Hilda Ogden is shortlisted for the job of community centre caretaker but the job goes to Gertie Robson.
★ Lucille Hewitt reveals she is living with mechanic Danny Burrows while Annie Walker thinks she is staying with Lorraine Binks.

APRIL
★ Lucille leaves Danny after Annie Walker invites him to tea and gives him the third degree.
★ Betty Turpin, unable to sell her house, takes up her old job at the Rovers again. Mavis Riley becomes a vet's receptionist.

MAY
★ Hilda Ogden lands a job on a cruise ship, *Monte Umbe*, and in her absence Stan takes in a couple of lodgers, Tommy Deakin and his nephew Michael Ryan, and is breathalysed for driving the Rolls that they have borrowed. The lodgers quit leaving Stan with their donkey, the main asset of their garden manure business.

JUNE
★ Hilda returns but when Stan tells her he faces a fine she refuses to bail him out of trouble.

★ Ron Cooke proposes marriage to Maggie Clegg. He says he has been dry for two years, has found a job in Zaire and wants her to accompany him. A jealous Alf Roberts also proposes but is rejected.

JULY
★ Young soldier Martin Downes arrives at the Rovers seeking his mother. He realises she is Bet Lynch but, appalled at her vulgarity, he leaves without revealing his identity.
★ Stan Ogden is fined £50 and £143 costs. Hilda pays and is left with just £7 from her cruise earnings, and when she asks Annie Walker for a rise is sacked.
★ Maggie marries Ron Cooke and sells the corner shop to the Welsh family Hopkins, headed by Granny, whose first act is to refuse credit to Hilda Ogden.

AUGUST
★ Stan and Hilda put their house up for sale after being offered the caretakership of the community centre, but the council withdraw their offer. Annie Walker gives Hilda her job back with a small pay increase.
★ Ken Barlow begins a new job as an executive at the warehouse and faces his first management test when the warehouse unions demand recognition.
★ Billy Walker and Deirdre Hunt fall in love after he has given her a lift.

▲ *Stan sees off Hilda as she gets herself a cleaning job on a cruise liner.*

▲ *Street residents turn out for Maggie Clegg's wedding to Ron Cooke, whose job in Zaire means that she follows him*

◀ *The Hopkins family – Granny, Idris, Vera and Tricia – arrive in the street and take over the shop*

SEPTEMBER
★ Landlord Wormold's assistant Jimmy Graham falls for Rita and offers to leave his wife for her but she does not trust him.

OCTOBER
★ The street girls win a package holiday to Majorca in a Spot the Ball contest. Mavis Riley meets a Spaniard, Rita falls for a bronzed beach bum, and Bet gets tied up with a property tycoon who turns out to be a conman, and misses the plane home. When Annie Walker gets back she finds Billy has been serving drinks after hours in the Rovers.
★ Billy is in the cells after servicing a van that contains jackets stolen from the warehouse, but Ken Barlow gets him out after obtaining a confession from one of the thieves.

NOVEMBER
★ Ernest and Emily Bishop decide to foster two black children whose father is in hospital.
★ Ken Barlow, in the middle of union negotiations, falls for union organiser Peggy Barton.

DECEMBER
★ Eddie Yeats, Jed Stone's Walton jail cellmate, arrives to spend Christmas with Minnie Caldwell in place of Jed, whose parole has been cancelled. Eddie cashes in on a power cut by selling cut price candles in the Rovers.
★ Granny Hopkins finds Gordon Clegg's birth certificate that shows his mother is actually Betty Turpin and tries to blackmail Maggie, home from Zaire for Christmas, into reducing the price of the shop. Maggie refuses and tells Gordon the truth.

1975

◄ *Mavis Riley finds love with Bet Lynch's Spanish neighbour Carlos, but when he proposes to her she realises he is seeking only a residency permit*

JANUARY
★ Eddie Yeats is taken back to Walton jail in a prison van for overstaying his Christmas parole.

★ Councillor Len Fairclough is held by murder squad detectives, after battered wife Lynn Johnson, who approached him for advice, is found dead in his living room. Len is released when her husband confesses to her murder.

FEBRUARY
★ Granny Hopkins sends Gordon Clegg an unpleasant letter revealing his parentage, but it comes as no shock because Maggie has already told him how she adopted Betty's baby. Gordon tears up the corner shop sale contract and the Hopkins family do a midnight flit.

MARCH
★ Len Fairclough is involved in a relationship with Bet Lynch.

★ Stan Ogden returns from hospital after middle ear trouble to find his social security benefit cut, so Hilda takes over his window cleaning round, and with the help of Eddie Yeats takes more cash than Stan normally did.

★ Betty Turpin is declared Newton and Ridley Pub Personality of the Year.

APRIL
★ Bet Lynch breaks off her affair with Len Fairclough, then learns that her illegitimate son Martin has been killed in a road accident in Belfast.

★ Stan Ogden and Eddie Yeats go into the guard dog business with a hound called Fury, which Albert Tatlock lets them keep in his back yard.

MAY
★ Fury is guarding Len Fairclough's yard when a thief breaks in, steals £200 worth of copper piping and the dog.

★ Deirdre Hunt backs out of her planned June wedding to Billy Walker and he goes to manage a hotel in Jersey.

JUNE
★ Ernest Bishop, who has formed WARP, the Weatherfield Association of Ratepayers, accuses Len Fairclough of corruption and is forced to apologise on local radio.

★ Ken Barlow tries his hand at taxi driving but Annie Walker objects to him using the Rovers telephone for bookings.

★ Deirdre resigns from her job at Len's yard after a blazing row with Ray Langton, but hate quickly turns to love.

JULY
★ After a joint stag and hen party at the Rovers, Ray and Deirdre marry at the register office. Len Fairclough throws a champagne party and the newly-weds miss their train and spend their wedding night with Deirdre's mother, Blanche.

★ Albert Tatlock goes to hospital to have a floating piece of shrapnel removed from his behind, and then parades round the Rovers showing off his World War One 'memento'.

★ Donna Parker, a Post Office canteen worker, calls on Alf Roberts late at night saying she has been thrown out of her flat. He lends her £500 to start a hairdressing business and she disappears with the cash.

AUGUST
★ The street holds a big party to celebrate Albert Tatlock's 80th birthday and his old regiment, the Lancashire Fusliers, send a bugler.

★ Ken Barlow enrols at a computer dating agency and is paired with Mavis Armitage – who turns out to be Mavis Riley.

SEPTEMBER
★ Cab driver Ken Barlow is hailed by his estranged wife Janet and Vince Denton, the man with whom she is living. Ken invites them home and they get on well together.

★ Newly-wed Deirdre Langton has a party and throws everyone out when someone leaves a cigarette smouldering on her new coffee table.

★ Eddie Yeats is arrested for handling stolen property.

★ Three young hooligans wreck the community centre and Ken Barlow goes to their homes to remonstrate. Unknown to him Albert Tatlock has reported them to the police and they smash Ken's windows, thinking he has shopped them.

OCTOBER
★ Three delinquents break into the warehouse and cause a fire with a discarded cigarette. The street has to be evacuated as flames approach liquid gas tanks. Edna Gee is missing and is discovered to have died in the fire.

★ When Annie Walker returns to the pub the next day her nest egg of 35 gold sovereigns is missing. All the customers are under suspicion until Billy Walker reveals he had put them away for safety.

NOVEMBER
★ Ken Barlow is appointed Community Development Officer at the community centre, but his first project, a Bonfire Night reading of the history of the gunpowder plot, attracts an audience of one boy.

★ Len Fairclough learns of the death through pneumonia of his partner Jerry Booth.

★ Annie Walker is terrorised by two yobs who have hidden in the pub at closing time, but Len and Ray chase them off.

DECEMBER
★ Deirdre blacks Tricia Hopkins' eye for spreading the word that Ray is having an affair with blonde housewife Pauline Jarvis.

★ The Rovers Amateur Dramatic Society Christmas show is *Cinderella* with Len as Buttons, Deirdre as Dandini, Bet as Prince Charming, and Tricia Hopkins playing the title role with a black eye.

▲ *Mavis Riley and Ken Barlow are matched when they join a computer dating agency*

▼ *The warehouse is ablaze after three youths break in and leave a cigarette smouldering*

1976

JANUARY
★ Blanche Hunt goes with Dave Smith to manage his new country club, leaving the corner shop in the hands of Betty Turpin.

FEBRUARY
★ Annie Walker is caught by the TV licence detector van; Hilda Ogden panics and goes to buy a licence, unknown to husband Stan who tries to hide the set and drops it.

MARCH
★ Ken Barlow is attracted to married graduate Wendy Nightingale, who is conducting a survey on reading habits at the community centre, and they spend a night together while her husband is away.
★ Mavis Riley returns from a mysterious weekend with Derek Wilton in Kendal, wearing a moonstone ring. She refuses to elaborate.
★ Stan Ogden and Albert Tatlock are accidentally locked in the cellar of the Rovers. Annie Walker, whose stock is depleted by them, engages Fred Gee as resident potman.

APRIL
★ Wendy Nightingale's husband goes to No 11 and assaults Ken Barlow. The centre committee tells Ken to regularise his private life.
★ Newton and Ridley run a Super-Brain contest and Stan Ogden wins the right to represent the Rovers. The other regulars do not give him much of a chance, so ply him with beer and send him to the wrong venue, fielding Bet Lynch as a substitute and she wins through to the finals.
★ Elsie Howard returns to the street and is made manageress of Sylvia's Separates.
★ Ernest Bishop is locked out by Emily after he goes on a strippers and booze evening with Alf Roberts and Ray Langton, forgetting that it is his wedding anniversary. The club is raided by police and the story is splashed across the front page of the *Weatherfield Gazette*.
★ Stan attempts an escapology act at a Spring bank holiday fête, but is unable to free himself.

MAY
★ Wendy Nightingale moves in with Ken, but goes back to her husband when the community centre committee threatens Ken with the sack. Ken gives in his notice.
★ Fred Gee falls for Rita Littlewood and gives her a single rose.
★ Renee Bradshaw makes Gordon Clegg an offer for the corner shop and takes it over for a three-week trial.

JUNE
★ Eddie Yeats returns looking for digs, and Ray Langton sends him to No 11. Elsie returns to find Eddie and his pal Monkey Gibbon sleeping in her bed, and attacks Ray with her handbag when she sees him in the Rovers.
★ Renee Bradshaw is reported for Sunday trading and accuses Emily Bishop of shopping her, though it was in fact Tricia Hopkins.

JULY
★ The Ogdens invite Eddie Yeats to lodge with them and in return he decorates the house. To fill a gap when he runs out of paper he buys a vista of the Alps, a 'muriel' which captures Hilda's heart.
★ Ernest Bishop is broke and Emily sells her engagement ring to pay bills.

AUGUST
★ Annie Walker is determined to learn to drive after hearing that her friend Nellie Harvey has passed the test after 86 lessons.
★ Ernest Bishop turns down a hospital porter's job because the sight of blood makes him faint, and becomes a pianist at stag

nights at the Gatsby. But Emily is upset when a stripper calls to practise.

★ Len's tools are stolen from a building site by labourer Jack Barker. Barker fixes scaffolding so that Len will fall, but it collapses under Ray and Len brawls with Barker in a fist fight.

SEPTEMBER

★ Gail Potter is cited as co-respondent in a divorce case and loses her job at Sylvia's Separates, but Elsie wins it back for her.

★ Fred Gee buys a greyhound and keeps it in Annie Walker's cellar.

★ Ken Barlow discovers that Eddie Yeats has an affinity with children and offers him a job as a playleader, but is forced to sack him when parents object to their children being supervised by a jailbird.

OCTOBER

★ Minnie Caldwell's house, No 5, is up for sale, six months after she left the street to keep house for old schoolfriend Handel Gartside in Whaley Bridge, Cheshire.

★ Mike Baldwin opens a new warehouse and goes into the shirt and jeans business, recruiting Ernest Bishop as his payroll clerk.

★ In a row with Len Fairclough at the Gatsby Club, Rita Littlewood knocks him from a bar stool and he falls, cracking his head. He feigns injury to receive attention but Rita pours a pint of beer over his head.

NOVEMBER

★ Stan Ogden is reported missing by Hilda but turns up at the chip shop run by his brother-in-law Norman Crabtree. Hilda drags him home.

★ Mike Baldwin buys No 5 and installs Bet Lynch nominally as his housekeeper.

★ Mavis Riley writes an earthy novel called 'Song of a Scarlet Summer' using characters with the same initials as local residents.

DECEMBER

★ Sylvia's Separates is put up for sale and Mike Baldwin buys it as a retail outlet, but tells Elsie that she is too old to sell trendy clothes and moves her to the factory as a supervisor.

★ When wages clerk Ernest Bishop refuses to switch pay day to Thursday the factory girls debag him at a Christmas party.

★ Annie Walker passes her driving test and buys a secondhand Rover 2000 from Eddie Yeats' crooked friend Lanky Potts. After a Licensed Victuallers lunch she is breathalysed and the crystals turn green, but a blood sample goes in her favour.

▼ *Eddie Yeats proves an ideal playleader at the community centre, until parents learn of his criminal record and Ken Barlow is forced to sack him*

1977

▲ *Rovers barmaid Betty Turpin becomes godmother to Ray and Deirdre Langton's daughter, Tracy*

JANUARY
★ Deirdre Langton has a baby, Tracy Lynette.
★ Suzie Birchall joins Gail Potter in Mike Baldwin's casuals shop, the Western Front.

FEBRUARY
★ Hilda Ogden, worried that the number 13 is unlucky, persuades Stan to change their house number to 12A, but the council makes them change it back.
★ Janet Barlow pleads with Ken to take her back. He refuses but allows her to stay the night and next morning finds her dead from a drug overdose.
★ Emily Bishop confronts Ernest with a Valentine card he has received from spinster Thelma James who has pursued him since they met at a dance.

MARCH
★ Mike Baldwin orders Bet Lynch to make herself scarce because his wife is arriving for a three-day stay, though Bet finds out the woman is not legally his wife. When Bet refuses to budge, Mike sells the house to the Langtons and Bet is forced to move into the flat above the corner shop where she ruins Renee's stock by accidentally turning off the freezer.
★ Len Fairclough proposes to Rita who first turns him down, then changes her mind.

APRIL
★ Len and Rita are married and honeymoon in Tenerife where she has a cabaret date.
★ Fred Gee and Alf Roberts take Mavis and Renee fishing. Renee loses her footing and falls in the water; Fred falls in after her trying to save his rod and when Alf and Mavis try to pull them out they end up in the water too.

MAY
★ Mavis Riley moves into the flat above the Kabin, and Len and Rita have their first major row because he wanted to let it for a higher rent.
★ Elsie Howard has a visitor, Elaine Dennett from Newcastle, who says she and Alan are in love and he wants a divorce from Elsie.

JUNE
★ For Jubilee Day the residents plan a tableau 'Britain Through the Ages', but on the day the float will not start because Stan Ogden left its lights on all night and drained the battery. Ken Barlow appears as Sir Edmund Hillary and Albert Tatlock as Sherpa Tensing.
★ Baby-sitting for the Langtons, Ena Sharples falls and hits her head; Ray and Deirdre return from London to find Ena in hospital and Tracy with the Bishops at No 3.
★ Mike Baldwin introduces a three-day week at the factory and shop steward Ivy Tilsley threatens to lead the workforce out on strike.

JULY
★ Bet and Renee fall for two con men who arrange to meet them at a non-existent address; in their absence £400 worth of stock disappears from the corner shop.
★ Two brewery painters working at the Rovers are sacked, draymen walk out in protest and there is no beer. Stan and Eddie brew their own in the bath but Hilda, worrying that this is illegal, pulls the plug.

AUGUST
★ Betty Turpin storms out of the Rovers after being accused of stealing £45.
★ Ken Barlow has to be winched to safety

► *It's the Queen's Silver Jubilee, and Bet Lynch and Hilda Ogden lead the street's celebrations*

by a helicopter after a hiking accident on Kinder Scout, Derbyshire.

SEPTEMBER
★ Annie Walker invites her friends to a sherry party to show off her new carpet – monogrammed AW – and finds that the carpet, which she bought from Eddie Yeats, is from a bingo hall and AW stands for Alhambra, Weatherfield.
★ Warehouse driver Steve Fisher is threatened with the sack by Mike Baldwin after he takes Gail and Suzie with him on a business trip to Southport and parks on the beach where the van sinks in the sand.

OCTOBER
★ Hilda Ogden wins a Second Honeymoon competition run by Loving Cup shandies with the slogan, 'Be a mistress as well as a wife, and your husband will be your boyfriend'.
★ A tipsy Alf Roberts proposes to Renee Bradshaw in the Gatsby and she accepts, but Alf, sobering up rapidly, talks his way out of it.
★ Deirdre Langton is molested under the viaduct but refuses to report the assault to the police and becomes unbalanced.

► *Hilda mistakenly thinks Mike Baldwin's factory party is fancy-dress and goes as Charlie Chaplin*

NOVEMBER
★ Stan and Hilda Ogden enjoy their Second Honeymoon prize – a night in Room 504 at a four star hotel, with £25 to spend.
★ Deirdre walks out on Ray and her baby and contemplates suicide on a motorway parapet, but a lorry driver who stops to ask directions brings her back to safety and she returns home.

DECEMBER
★ Fred Gee, thinking that Len is two-timing Rita, knocks him out at Deirdre's New Year Eve party, breaking her precious coffee table.

1978

▼ *The Rovers is challenged to a sponsored pram race by the Flying Horse. Eddie and Mavis soon give up*

JANUARY

★ Hilda Ogden camps out all night at a January sale hoping to buy a colour television set for £5, but is so keen to be interviewed by local radio she loses her place in the queue, and her bargain.

★ Ernest Bishop is shot in a wages snatch at the warehouse, and dies on the operating table in hospital.

FEBRUARY

★ Ken Barlow dates divorcee chiropodist Sally Robson.

★ Gail, Suzie and Elsie panic because they think they have rats in the rafters but they turn out to be pigeons which have got through a hole in the Ogdens' roof. When Suzie's foot slips through the Ogden's ceiling, Hilda retaliates by pushing a broom handle through Elsie's.

MARCH

★ Alf and Renee are married and honeymoon on Capri while Len spends a night in jail for being drunk and disorderly after Alf's stag party.

★ Ernest Bishop's killers are jailed for life.

★ Elsie Howard has a night on the town after receiving her decree nisi.

APRIL

★ Len Fairclough is dropped as Ratepayers' Party candidate after his episode in the cells, while Rita locks him out of her bedroom because of the way he chatted up a policewoman.

MAY

★ Ken organises a Bank Holiday night at the Rovers while Annie Walker is away, but police investigating the theft of her Rover car (later recovered) book everyone for drinking after hours.

JUNE

★ Fred Gee, keen to have his own pub, is told by the brewery that he can have the Mechanics Arms, provided he has a wife, but his marriage proposals are turned down by Bet Lynch, Betty Turpin and Alma Walsh, the Flying Horse barmaid.

★ Hilda Ogden demands a new brush from Mike Baldwin and is sacked for damaging the old one. The workers walk out and picket the factory.

★ Elsie Howard says she wishes to be known as Elsie Tanner again.

JULY

★ Mike Baldwin is forced to offer Hilda her job back again.

★ Ena Sharples needs a new bed but cannot afford one, so Eddie, Len, Ray and Emily break into her house and install a new one. Ena is not pleased, claiming that her life savings were in the mattress of the one they took away.

AUGUST

★ Baker Joe Dawson opens a café next to the Kabin and employs Emily as manageress.

★ Hilda Ogden, annoyed by her high water rates bill, tells Stan to bath daily in order to get value for money, but the bath overflows and ruins her 'muriel' which she replaces with a seascape.

SEPTEMBER

★ Albert Tatlock blames an outbreak of food poisoning on Annie Walker's pies, but the cause is traced to his own allotment where he has sprayed vegetables with an insecticide.

★ Elsie Tanner develops a relationship with taxi driver Ron Mather.

OCTOBER

★ Deirdre confronts Ray Langton about his dates with Janice Stubbs, a waitress from Dawson's café.

NOVEMBER

★ Deirdre's marriage is on the rocks; Ray takes a contract building job in Holland, leaving her and daughter Tracy at No 5.

★ Mike Baldwin decides that business is too slow at his Western Front casuals shop and closes it. Suzie Birchall leaves for London.

DECEMBER

★ Deirdre gets an ultimatum from Ray – to join him in Holland or put their house up for sale.

★ Brian Tilsley gatecrashes a Christmas party at Elsie Tanner's house and makes a date with Gail Potter.

★ Ken Barlow gives reading lessons to illiterate Karen Barnes, ignoring advice that her husband can be jealous and violent.

▼ *To Stan's bemusement, Hilda takes up art as a hobby*

1979

JANUARY

★ Hilda Ogden takes up painting and Eddie Yeats tries to con Annie Walker into paying 20 guineas for one of her pictures, but Annie finds a message on the back that reads: 'Stan – am at bingo. Your dinner's in the oven.'

★ Dave Barnes bursts in on Ken Barlow's lessons to his wife Karen and threatens Ken and Albert, but Ken knocks him cold, more by accident than judgement.

★ Bert and Ivy Tilsley buy No 5 Coronation Street from Deirdre for £7,000.

★ Suzie Birchall returns from London and signs with a modelling agency.

FEBRUARY

★ Rita Fairclough sings at the Gatsby while Len recuperates from a collapse brought on by overwork.

★ Bert and Ivy moves into No 5 and Stan Ogden cleans their windows by mistake. When Ivy refuses to pay, Hilda throws a bucket of dirty water over her.

★ Brian Tilsley begins relationship with Gail Potter.

★ Elsie's friend Ron Mather leaves to take a chauffeur's job in Torquay.

MARCH

★ A lorry ploughs into the Rovers after its driver dies from a heart attack. Deirdre is hysterical because Tracy's pram was seen parked outside shortly before and her doll is found in the rubble, but the baby is found to be safe with Sally Norton who was wheeling Tracy. Alf Roberts is unconscious in hospital for three weeks, and Mike Baldwin and Len Fairclough are also hurt.

★ When Mike Baldwin puts officious young Steve Fisher in charge of the factory, the girls threaten to walk out, and Mike discharges himself from hospital to sort out the trouble.

APRIL

★ Brian Tilsley and Gail Potter become engaged despite his mother's objections that Gail is not a Catholic.

★ Fred Gee, encouraged by Audrey Potter, buys a wig.

MAY

★ Eddie and Stan are keeping three hens in the Ogdens' back garden and Hilda Ogden gives two eggs to Ena, not realising they are hard boiled and have been placed in the coop by Suzie Birchall as a prank.

★ Alf Roberts is given to outbursts of ill temper since leaving hospital. He insults customers in the shop and is sent for psychiatric treatment.

★ Ken Barlow invites Deirdre Langton to a disco but meets competition from Billy Walker.

JUNE

★ Eddie Yeats buys a metal detector in the hope of finding buried riches; Albert Tatlock gets his allotment dug over by telling Eddie and the Ogdens he has found ancient coins on his plot.

▲ An hysterical Deirdre Langton fears for daughter Tracy when a lorry crashes into the Rovers

▼ *Gail Potter's mother Audrey meets Suzie Birchall at Gail and Brian Tilsley's engagement party*

JULY
★ The Faircloughs row after Rita and Bet, on a caravan holiday in Morecambe, meet two men at a party and let them stay the night because they have lost the keys to their own van.

AUGUST
★ Ivy invites Brian and Gail to live with them at No 5 after they are married and Gail is uneasy about her domineering future mother-in-law.

SEPTEMBER
★ When the factory burglar alarm disturbs a quiet Sunday morning Stan Ogden whacks it with a poker and causes an electrical fault that blacks out the street.

OCTOBER
★ Ken and Deirdre return from a holiday in the Lake District; next day Deirdre gets a letter from Ray, threatening to cite Ken as co-respondent in a divorce case.

NOVEMBER
★ Brian and Gail marry, with her mother, Audrey Potter, as matron of honour.

DECEMBER
★ Elsie Tanner is invited by Ron Mather to join him in Torquay and seeks to sell her house. But after a visit to Torquay, Elsie announces she is staying in the street.
★ Suzie Birchall is sacked by Mike Baldwin for ringing her punk boyfriend on the office phone.

1980

JANUARY

★ Jim Sedgewick takes over Dawson's and turns it into a transport café with a juke box; an annoyed Emily Bishop walks out and Elsie Tanner replaces her as manageress.

FEBRUARY

★ Ken Barlow expresses reluctance to marry Deirdre Langton because he feels he is too old to risk a third marriage.
★ Len finds Rita – who walked out after a blazing row – working in a Blackpool launderette but she declines to return to Weatherfield.

MARCH

★ Annie upsets her staff at the Rovers by installing a bell with which to summon them.
★ Fred Gee chauffeurs Annie Walker and her guest, Olive Taylor-Brown, to a ladies' evening but leaves her handbag containing the tickets on the car roof and a humiliated Annie is refused admission.

APRIL

★ In a ballot for shop steward at the factory, Ivy Tilsley scrapes home by three votes over Ida Clough.
★ Ena Sharples leaves for a new life at St Anne's-on-Sea, near Blackpool.
★ When the Rovers enters a barber-shop quartet competition Fred Gee is sacked for singing flat and Renee is substituted, but the Flying Horse wins.

MAY

★ Brian and Gail have mortgage problems and Ivy gives them £300 that she has saved for her holiday.
★ Rita returns to Weatherfield to work in the Kabin.
★ Pet shop owner Arnold Swain, a client of Emily Bishop's new typing agency, asks her for a date, her first since Ernest's death.
★ Bet Lynch shows her new live-in lover, lorry driver Dan Johnson, the door for assaulting one of her neighbours.

▲ *Alf Roberts prepares for wife Renee's funeral after her fatal car accident*

▲ *Happiness turns to heartbreak when Emily finds that second husband Arnold Swain is already married*

JUNE
★ Ivy Tilsley is promoted factory supervisor.
★ Arnold Swain proposes to Emily Bishop but she turns him down, asking to remain friends.
★ Gail forgets to take the Pill and becomes pregnant.

JULY
★ Hilda Ogden wins a raffle, the prize a date with 'Mr Wonderful', and finds out that the mystery man is Mike Baldwin, who offers her £40 to call it off.
★ Alf and Renee Roberts sell the corner shop to start a new life, but driving home after a celebratory pub lunch, Renee stalls the car at traffic lights and a lorry ploughs into it. She dies in hospital.
★ Elsie Tanner sets an armchair on fire after falling asleep with a lighted cigarette; Hilda Ogden, calling round to borrow a cup of sugar, raises the alarm and saves her life.

AUGUST
★ Brian and Gail Tilsley fall for a salesman's chat and buy a new 'micro bijou residence'.

SEPTEMBER
★ Emily Bishop and Arnold Swain marry at the register office.
★ Bet Lynch loses her handbag at the sales; a hoaxer telephones to invite her to collect it, and while she is out her flat is stripped by burglars.

OCTOBER
★ Elsie's grandson, Martin Cheveski, and his girlfriend Karen continue dating despite her father's disapproval.
★ Brian Tilsley is sacked by the garage for taking his mother-in-law out in a client's car.

NOVEMBER
★ Annie Walker demands a different refuse collection team, as a result of which all Weatherfield's binmen boycott the Rovers and Annie is forced to apologise.

DECEMBER
★ Stan Ogden is told by his doctor that he may be allergic to beer and goes on the wagon until it is established that his allergy is to eggs.
★ Mike Baldwin's tricky father Frankie disappears to London with £70 that Fred Gee has invested in a video project.
★ Arnold Swain is exposed as a bigamist and Emily sends him packing.
★ Gail Tilsley gives birth to a 7lb 2oz boy.

1981

JANUARY
★ Gail changes her baby's names from David Daniel to Nicholas Paul, to avoid the initials DDT.
★ Mike Baldwin's father Frankie repays Fred Gee but reveals that the vice squad are on his trail. His cheque bounces.
★ Ken Barlow buys a Volkswagen Beetle, but Albert Tatlock refuses to ride in 'a Jerry car'.

FEBRUARY
★ Annie Walker goes on a cruise and the Rovers is taken over by disciplinarian Gordon Lewis. Fred is suspended for drinking whisky without paying for it, and Betty Turpin is accused of giving short change.
★ Elsie Tanner makes a play for beefy trucker Wally Randle, a customer at the café.

MARCH
★ Ken attends Mike Baldwin's flat-warming party with beautician Sonia Price, but Mike whisks her off to a nightclub, leaving Ken with Deirdre.
★ Annie Walker returns from holiday to find her staff replaced by newcomers but returns things to normal.
★ Arnold Swain returns to terrorise Emily, and is committed to a mental home, while she goes on a holiday to Malta with Mavis Riley.

APRIL
★ Still seeking his own pub, which he has been promised if he is married, Fred proposes to Eunice Nuttall.
★ Wally Randle gives Elsie the brush-off and, feeling her advancing years, she takes home rough and ready Bill Fielding for the night. Next day, she is visited by Fielding's wife, who slashes Elsie's clothes.

MAY
★ Fred and Eunice are married at the register office.
★ Brian Tilsley's pal, Colin Jackson, makes advances to Gail who kicks him out.

JUNE
★ Fred Gee's application for a pub is turned down because Eunice was once sacked from a barmaiding job for stealing.
★ Rita Fairclough is keen to adopt a child but Len will not hear of it; instead they agree to become foster parents.

JULY
★ Ken and Deirdre are married and honeymoon in Corfu.
★ Decorator Marcus Dodds starts work at the Rovers; he is an amateur artist and persuades Mavis Riley to pose nude for him but they both have second thoughts.
★ Elsie is offered a new job as a machinist at the factory.

▶ *Unwelcome advances from husband Brian's friend Colin Jackson force Gail Tilsley to give him his marching orders*

▼ *Young John Spencer becomes Len and Rita Fairclough's foster child while his mother is ill*

AUGUST
★ Fred and Eunice move out of the Rovers into her father's flat.
★ Len and Rita foster teenager John Spencer while his mother is in hospital.
★ Brian Tilsley gets a warning from Gail for an affair with flirty garage client Glenda Fox.

SEPTEMBER
★ Fred and Eunice become caretakers of the community centre.
★ Mike's father Frankie returns with money and a glamorous secretary on his arm.

OCTOBER
★ Brian Tilsley is charged with unlawful wounding after tackling a filling station robber and putting the boy on the critical list in hospital.
★ Audrey Potter starts giving discreet shampoos and sets in the back of the corner shop while Alf Roberts is away; Alf turns a blind eye.

NOVEMBER
★ Brian is cleared of the assault charge.
★ Audrey Potter persuades an infatuated Alf to buy her a car but when he proposes marriage she hesitates, and goes back to her old boyfriend.
★ Fred Gee is asked to leave the community centre for being rude to the public.

DECEMBER
★ The Gees are offered work at a private hotel. Eunice accepts but Fred refuses and goes back to his old job at the Rovers. Their marriage appears to be over.
★ Emily Bishop hears that Arnold Swain has died and left her £2,000.
★ Annie Walker introduces a cocktail hour at the Rovers in a desire for greater sophistication.

1982

JANUARY
★ Emily Bishop spends Arnold's legacy on gifts for the hospital and local children, then gives £2,000 of her own money to Arnold's penniless widow, Margaret.
★ Brian Tilsley goes to work in Qatar in the Persian Gulf with businessman Roy Sykes.
★ Betty Turpin receives a visit from her son, Gordon Clegg, and his fiancée Caroline Wilson.

FEBRUARY
★ Eddie Yeats becomes a CB radio enthusiast with the call sign Slim Jim, and makes contact on the air with Stardust Lil, otherwise Marion Willis. To impress her he borrows the keys to Mike Baldwin's luxury flat from cleaner Hilda Ogden.

MARCH
★ The Faircloughs' new foster-child, 16 year old Sharon Gaskell, is good at woodwork and keen on football.
★ Gail is upset when Brian prefers to spend his leave in Cairo rather than Weatherfield.
★ Betty Turpin's former lodger, travelling electrician Alec Hobson, moves back in with her.

APRIL
★ A bored Gail returns to her old job at the café while neighbour Jackie baby-sits.
★ Mavis Riley's old flame Derek Wilton brings her flowers.
★ Jack Duckworth has a night out with Bet Lynch. When Vera finds out she collects Jack's clothes and dumps them at the Rovers.

MAY
★ Eddie Yeats confesses his prison record to Marion, but she accepts his proposal and they hold a rowdy engagement party.
★ Mike Baldwin recruits Emily Bishop as wages clerk at the factory.
★ Betty Turpin is mugged by a youngster from Ken Barlow's youth club.

JUNE
★ Toddler Nicky Tilsley goes missing and a big search is launched before he is found, locked in Len Fairclough's new house.

◀ *Eddie Yeats introduces fiancée Marion Willis to Stan and Hilda Ogden. Their CB radio antics brought them together and they eventually marry, despite Marion calling off the engagement*

► *Bossy Phyllis Pearce keeps an eye on binman Chalkie Whiteley, grandfather and guardian to Craig Whiteley, who is also her grandson*

JULY
★ Maggie Dunlop comforts Mike Baldwin after the death of his father and he invites her to move in with him.
★ Brian Tilsley, home from the Gulf, is surprised when Gail's new admirer Les Charlton calls in, and Brian decides to stay home.
★ The Faircloughs move into their new house, and binman Chalkie Whiteley moves into their old one.

AUGUST
★ With his earnings from Qatar, Brian Tilsley goes into partnership in a garage with Ron Sykes.

SEPTEMBER
★ Mike Baldwin breaks up with girlfriend Maggie Dunlop.
★ Sharon Gaskell baby-sits for the Tilsleys and tries to seduce Brian.

OCTOBER
★ Hilda Ogden has a new job, cleaning for Dr and Mrs Lowther, and bores friends with stories of their luxurious lifestyle.

NOVEMBER
★ Mavis Riley joins a writing class and meets Victor Pendlebury who invites her to collaborate on a short story for local radio.
★ Marion Willis breaks off her engagement to Eddie Yeats when he loses their savings on a dubious car import scheme.

DECEMBER
★ Sharon accepts a kennelmaid's job in Sheffield, and leaves the street.
★ Marion changes her mind, launches a CB radio search for Eddie, and they have a loving reunion on Liverpool docks.
★ Mike Baldwin threatens to sack Ivy Tilsley when he discovers the factory workers are making handbags on the side.
★ Deirdre has a row with Ken and spends a cosy evening with Mike at his flat.

▲ *Calm before the storm, as Albert Tatlock hugs Ken and Deirdre Barlow's daughter, Tracy*

1983

◄ *Ken Barlow remonstrates with smooth-talking Mike Baldwin over his affair with wife Deirdre. Ken orders her to leave, but she cannot walk out on him and they fall back into each other's arms*

JANUARY
★ Deirdre tells husband Ken she is meeting a girlfriend but spends another cosy evening with Mike.

★ Annie Walker's cherished Rover is written off when Eddie Yeats backs his dustcart into it.

FEBRUARY
★ Suzie Birchall returns to Weatherfield and Fred Gee gets her relief work at the Rovers.

★ Mike presses Deirdre to leave Ken and marry him, but, confronted by Ken, Deirdre agrees to give their marriage a second chance. Ken books a holiday in Malta and warns Mike off.

MARCH
★ Stan Ogden is too ill to continue his window cleaning round and is in debt to moneylender Syd Kippax. Eddie Yeats clears the debt by buying Stan's round and becomes his boss.

★ Brian Tilsley takes a bank loan and becomes sole owner of the garage. His father, Bert, tells Brian he has had a slight stroke, but asks him not to tell Ivy.

APRIL
★ Elsie Tanner turns her front parlour into a bed-sit for Marion Willis.

★ Mike, Len and Alf join forces to open a local wine bar and disco, the Graffiti Club.

★ Mavis spends her 46th birthday camping in the Lake District with Victor Pendlebury.

★ Suzie Birchall has a visit from her husband; after he has left, Elsie finds Suzie has been beaten up.

MAY
★ Pam Mitchell of the *Weatherfield Recorder* invites Ken Barlow to write an advice column.

★ Bet goes to a video dating agency and is surprised to be shown a tape of Vince St Clair, who is actually Jack Duckworth. Bet persuades Vera to join the club as Carole Munro and arrange a date with 'Vince'.

JUNE
★ Mavis, offered a trial marriage by Victor, is furious to hear herself referred to by his neighbour as 'Mrs Pendlebury'.

★ Hilda inherits her late brother Archie's chip shop, but sells it after a row with Archie's common-law wife, spending the money on new carpets and a bidet.

JULY
★ Bert Tilsley, helping out at Brian's garage while Brian is giving a driving lesson, is hurt in a tyre explosion and lies unconscious in hospital.

★ Bet Lynch starts a slimming contest at the Rovers, from which Fred Gee is disqualified after he is found to have filled his pockets with copper coins before the first weigh-in.

AUGUST

★ Chalkie Whiteley sells his house for £10,000 and emigrates to Australia. The Duckworths move in.

★ Bert Tilsley goes missing after being discharged from hospital and is traced to Bristol, suffering from a mental breakdown.

★ Ken Barlow takes voluntary redundancy from the Town Hall after leaking to the *Recorder* council plans to close down youth clubs.

★ Percy Sugden is appointed caretaker of the community centre.

SEPTEMBER

★ Terry Duckworth asks Fred Gee to prove he was a paratrooper and Fred injures his back leaping off a wall.

OCTOBER

★ Brian and Gail sell their home and move in with Ivy.

★ Betty Turpin objects to new Rovers staff uniforms which, she says, look like 'sprayed on T-shirts'.

★ Marion Willis is pregnant and she and Eddie decide to marry. Fred taunts Eddie, they fight, and the groom arrives at the church with a black eye.

★ Deirdre is shocked to discover that Ken has put his redundancy money into a partnership in the *Recorder*.

NOVEMBER

★ Emily Bishop takes in bookish dustman Curly Watts as a lodger.

★ Hilda wants to go abroad to celebrate her ruby wedding anniversary and applies for a copy of Stan's birth certificate to get him a passport. They then discover he is 64, not 61 as they had thought.

DECEMBER

★ Eddie and Marion leave for a new life in Bury, Lancashire.

★ Rita Fairclough learns that Len has been killed in a motorway crash; after the funeral she discovers he was on his way back from a night out with another woman.

▼ *Grief and disbelief for Rita Fairclough when Len dies in a motorway car crash after a date with another woman*

1984

◀ *Bill Webster and Elaine Prior discuss their future together*

JANUARY
★ Elsie Tanner's old flame, Bill Gregory, wines and dines her and persuades her to join him in a new life in Portugal.
★ Bert Tilsley dies in hospital.

FEBRUARY
★ Stan gets £200 compensation after stubbing his toe on a paving stone and Ken publishes a picture of the digit in the *Recorder*.
★ Bill Webster rents Len Fairclough's old yard and sets up as a property developer.

MARCH
★ In Annie Walker's absence, Billy returns to take over the Rovers and upsets everyone.
★ Bill Webster borrows £1,000 from Rita to finance his business and Alf Roberts is jealous.
★ Ivy has an admirer, Arthur Whittaker, but she tells him she is not ready for a serious relationship yet.

APRIL
★ The Rovers gets another stand-in manager, Frank Harvey, who invites Bet to a brewery dance when the new barmaid turns him down; in revenge Bet turns up as a tramp.

MAY
★ Gordon Lewis takes over at the Rovers and reintroduces a disciplined regime; the staff are soon in revolt.

★ Albert Tatlock's daughter Beattie arrives to say her father has died. She gives his Military Medal to Ken.
★ The Duckworths are fined £150 for not having a TV licence after a visit from a detector van. Drinking to celebrate the fact that the fine was less than he feared, Jack falls over the TV set and smashes it.

JUNE
★ Taught by Brian, Mavis passes her driving test and then reverses into Jack Duckworth's taxi.
★ Bill Webster buys Elsie Tanner's house and persuades her daughter Linda to move out.
★ Amateur astronomer Curly Watts is interviewed by local radio after seeing a UFO in the night sky.

JULY
★ Billy Walker, pressed by creditors, seeks to borrow £6,000.

AUGUST
★ Derek Wilton wines and dines Mavis and they become engaged but Victor Pendlebury gatecrashes the party and says he loves her too.
★ Billy Walker returns to run the Rovers again and goads Fred Gee into thumping him so that he can sack him.
★ Gail takes over management of the café, against the wishes of Brian and Ivy.

SEPTEMBER
★ After a robbery at the corner shop Percy Sugden organises a street home-watch; too vigilant, he is arrested as a peeping Tom.
★ The day of Mavis's wedding to Derek arrives but she decides she does not love him – just as Derek also decides not to go through with it.

◀ *Bet Lynch, Hilda Ogden and Vera Duckworth line up for the egg-and-spoon race in the Pub Olympics contest between the Rovers Return and the Flying Horse*

▶ *Busybody Percy Sugden gets into the spirit of things as he does his farmyard impersonations*

OCTOBER

★ Ken Barlow falls in love with his *Weatherfield Recorder* assistant Sally Waterman.

★ Jack Duckworth, breathalysed after celebrating Vera's £260 bingo win, is banned from driving for a year and loses his taxi driving job; he starts selling shirts on the market.

★ Betty Turpin takes in Police Sgt Tony Cunliffe as a lodger.

NOVEMBER

★ Hilda collapses under the strain of nursing sick Stan and he is sent to hospital where he dies. Hilda orders a tombstone with space for two names.

DECEMBER

★ Vera buys Stan's window cleaning round and puts Jack to work. He decides the job has its moments when he meets sultry customer Dulcie Froggatt. Vera puts his exhaustion down to overwork.

★ Billy Walker is stripped of the tenancy of the Rovers by the brewery and returns to Jersey. Bet, Jack and Gordon Lewis all apply to take over.

★ Percy Sugden's niece, Elaine Prior, falls for Bill Webster and they plan to marry and move to Southampton. Bill's son, Kevin, elects to stay in Weatherfield.

★ Rita ends a brief romance with Police Sgt Tony Cunliffe, unable to get over Len's death.

1985

▲ *Bet Lynch celebrates her new position as Rovers landlady with the Lady Victuallers*

JANUARY
★ The brewery awards the tenancy of the Rovers to Bet; Gordon Lewis gets another pub as consolation.
★ Kevin Webster is allowed to live in his father's house until it is sold.
★ Mike Baldwin has an affair with designer Christine Millward until her husband appears.

FEBRUARY
★ Old soldier Percy Sugden organises a Valentine's Day dance for charity at the community centre and is appalled when the disc jockey, known as Kaiser Bill, appears wearing a German helmet.
★ The name of Elizabeth Theresa Lynch appears over the Rovers door.

MARCH
★ Gail is tired of life with her interfering mother-in-law and wants a home of her own, but Brian is happy to continue living with mother.

APRIL
★ Gail walks out on Brian and rents a slummy bed-sit, taking little Nicky with her, at which Brian agrees to apply for a council house.

★ Jack gives Vera a length of silver lurex material to have made up into a dress by Connie Clayton. Vera sees herself as the next Joan Collins.

MAY
★ A dispute between the Duckworths and the Claytons arises when Vera refuses to pay a £38 bill for the dress. Terry agrees to settle the bill because it threatens to jeopardise his affair with Andrea Clayton.
★ Kevin Webster falls for upper-class Michelle Robinson.

JUNE
★ Bet, Rita and Mavis have a get-away-from-it-all holiday in Blackpool and meet three men – but only Mavis's date is single.

JULY
★ After a holiday together, factory van driver George Wardle proposes to Ivy Tilsley and she accepts.
★ Andrea Clayton is pregnant by Terry Duckworth.
★ Planning to extend his shop, Alf Roberts offers Hilda £15,000 for her house next door. She is interested but then hedges, and Alf is furious to find out that she is being advised by Mike.

AUGUST
★ Hilda is under more pressure to sell when builder Les Pringle tells her that roof repairs may cost £2,000, but she does not want to move and Alf settles for converting the shop into a 'mini-market'.

SEPTEMBER
★ Frank Mills, a barman from Bet's holiday hotel in Blackpool, angles for a permanent job at the Rovers and entices Bet on a cruise to discuss it. Betty Turpin, running the Rovers in Bet's absence, engages barmaid Gloria Todd.
★ Phyllis Pearce has an admirer, pensioner Sam Tindall, but her eyes are on Percy Sugden.
★ With his Mini-Market open, Alf proposes to Rita Fairclough. She turns him down.
★ Terry Duckworth plans a new start by taking over Len Fairclough's old yard.

OCTOBER
★ The brewery is dissatisfied with Bet's management of the Rovers, and she is given three months to improve matters.
★ Percy Sugden is inveigled into joining Phyllis Pearce on a trip to Southport, and they miss the coach back.
★ Ivy Tilsley, intending to marry in church, is shocked when George Wardle reveals he is a divorcee and she calls the wedding off.
★ Tracy Barlow, brooding because her mother will not let her have a dog, goes missing for six hours and reappears with Ken Barlow's daughter Susan.

NOVEMBER
★ Jack Duckworth falls off his ladder, breaking an ankle, and is visited in hospital by Vera and Dulcie Froggatt.
★ Audrey Potter makes herself indispensable to Alf Roberts with the aim of becoming Mrs Roberts.

DECEMBER
★ Ivy Tilsley, though still troubled by her Catholic conscience, is preparing to marry George Wardle in a register office.
★ Audrey bends Alf Roberts' sports car but instead of suing, Alf proposes to her. Mike Baldwin is best man at their wedding.
★ Susan Barlow is enjoying her new job selling advertising space on Ken's newspaper, but her father is worried about her developing friendship with Mike Baldwin.

▲ *Audrey Potter decides to become a one-man woman and marries Alf Roberts*

1986

▼ *Garage mechanic Kevin Webster makes a splash with Sally Seddon and love follows*

JANUARY

★ Susan Barlow persists with her romance with Mike, even though her desperate father tells her of Mike's previous affair with Deirdre. Ken thumps Mike on the jaw.

★ Teenager Jenny Bradley's mother dies and Rita agrees to give her a home until Jenny's estranged father Alan can make arrangements.

★ Kevin Webster, driving at speed through wet streets in his van, accidentally soaks Sally Seddon, waiting at a bus stop; his apology leads to a relationship.

FEBRUARY

★ Audrey Roberts, tired of living over Alf's shop, tries to persuade him to buy a new £42,000 house in Bolton Road, but Alf prefers No 11 Coronation Street.

★ Susan Barlow leaves home and moves in with Mike. They plan to marry but Ken refuses to give his blessing.

MARCH

★ Alan Bradley is trying to mend fences with his daughter Jenny, whom he abandoned when she was six.

★ Curly Watts decides to give up his dustcart and work with Terry Duckworth on contracts for Mike Baldwin.

APRIL

★ The Barlow twins, Susan and Peter, are 21 and Peter, who is in the Royal Navy, brings his girlfriend Jessica to a party given by Ken Barlow. Terry Duckworth makes a play for Jessica and a scrap follows.

★ Gloria Todd is fearful when ex-boyfriend Steve Holt comes out of prison and moves into her flat.

MAY

★ Mike and Susan marry. Ken reluctantly gives the bride away.

★ Ivy Tilsley's nephew Ian Latimer visits from Australia and falls for Gail. They become lovers while Brian is on a business trip to Edinburgh.

JUNE

★ Ian Latimer flies back to Australia, seen off by a tearful Gail begging him to take her with him.

★ Vera Duckworth, who has won a car in a competition, books her first driving lessons, though Jack tells her she will never make a driver and might as well hand the car over to him.

★ Kevin Webster and Sally Seddon return from a pop concert in the early hours to see flames in the Rovers. Sally raises the alarm while Kevin rescues Bet. The fire, which badly damages the pub, is blamed on an electrical fault.

▲ *A fire engulfs the Rovers and Kevin rescues Bet Lynch from the flames*

◀ *Phyllis Pearce looks on as Brian and Gail Tilsley's marriage begins to crumble*

JULY
★ Alan Bradley is wooing both Gloria Todd and Rita Fairclough. When his two-timing is discovered, Gloria tells him to get out of her life.

AUGUST
★ Mavis Riley is trying to cope alone at the Kabin while Rita is on holiday when she is visited by Derek Wilton and, though she discovers he is now married, she finds herself attracted again.

★ Gail Tilsley confesses to Brian that she is expecting a baby and it could be Ian Latimer's. Brian leaves her and moves back home with his mother, Ivy.

★ Alf Roberts closes Audrey's front parlour hairdressing salon after she leaves a colour rinse too long on Hilda's hair and turns it orange – which costs Alf £25 in compensation to Hilda.

★ Hilda Ogden cuts the ribbon to re-open the rebuilt Rovers Return.

SEPTEMBER
★ Brian tells Gail he will return to her if she has an abortion but she refuses and he sees a solicitor about a divorce.

★ Mike Baldwin sacks Vera Duckworth for publicly abusing his wife Susan, whom Vera believed shopped her for being absent from the factory when she should have been working.

★ Alan Bradley has a date with Rita but stands her up because he has been made redundant and goes to Dubai in search of a new job.

OCTOBER
★ Kevin Webster and Sally Seddon marry after their landlady, Hilda Ogden, reads their tea leaves and promises them happiness.

★ Gail and Brian are at loggerheads over Brian's intention to take their son Nicky away for a weekend and Brian threatens to stop paying Gail's rent unless she signs divorce papers.

NOVEMBER
★ Emily Bishop gives £440 to Curly Watts to pay off the hire purchase debt on his cherished telescope, which has been stolen along with her jewellery, after she let two bogus water board men into the house.

★ The Rovers has not been doing well since it re-opened after the fire and the brewery is dissatisfied. Bet agrees to try booking one of Alec Gilroy's professional cabaret acts.

DECEMBER
★ Susan Baldwin, who has convinced Mike to give her a job at the factory, tries to persuade him to manufacture Hopscotch, a range of children's wear designed by an old college friend, Cheryl Crossley.

★ Martin Platt, who works at the café, drives Jenny to Rochdale in Rita's car to take part in a talent contest, which she wins. When she persuades him to let her take the wheel of the car she crashes and Martin is injured, but they both tell the police he was driving.

★ Tom Hopwood, Sally Webster's uncle, meets Hilda when he visits the newly-weds and takes her to see his allotment.

1987

JANUARY
★ Gail Tilsley receives the decree nisi, due to be made absolute in six weeks.
★ Alf's Mini-Market is broken into. Terry Duckworth confesses to the crime, but his mother, Vera, gives Alf £100 not to prosecute.

FEBRUARY
★ Ian Latimer arrives from Australia to ask Gail to marry him, after hearing about her pregnancy from Audrey, but she refuses, and then gives birth prematurely to a daughter, Sarah Louise.
★ Alan Bradley moves in with Rita Fairclough at No 7 and begins giving orders at the Kabin, clearing out records to make room for a video library.

MARCH
★ Alf Roberts takes exception to an article by Ken Barlow in the *Weatherfield Recorder* criticising independent councillors. Ken plans to stand as a Labour candidate against Alf, but Bob Statham, senior partner in the newspaper, tells him to stop playing politics – or stop editing.
★ After an audit of the accounts of the Rovers, the brewery decides to offer the tenancy for sale. Bet is unable to raise a £12,000 bank loan, but Alec Gilroy offers to lend her the money, and begins to throw his weight around in the pub.
★ Hilda Ogden's romance with Tom Hopwood hits a sticky patch when he abandons her to dance with Phyllis Pearce at an Over 60s tea dance, and Hilda sulks.

APRIL
★ Gail tells Brian he is the father of baby Sarah after all. Blood tests have shown that Ian Latimer could not be. Brian, who has moved in with Liz Turnbull, says nothing is changed.
★ Deirdre Barlow – egged on by Ken – is standing against Alf Roberts in the council elections and campaigns vigorously.

MAY
★ On polling day Deirdre triumphs. Alf attends her celebration party but leaves early, has a heart attack and is rushed to hospital.
★ Kevin and Sally have a home of their own at last. They move into the flat above Alf's mini-market, where she works.
★ Terry Duckworth is spending much of his time with his old army pal, Pete Jackson, and Pete's wife Linda is angry when Terry brings him home drunk.

JUNE
★ Pete Jackson catches Linda with Terry. He asks her not to leave him but Linda and Terry leave the area together.
★ Bet disappears – with the money Alec Gilroy lent her to buy the tenancy of the Rovers, and he asks the brewery to let him have the pub.
★ Jeff Singleton, a joiner, arrives to do some work on the café. He and Gail are attracted to each other and go out on a date.

JULY
★ Alan Bradley arranges to meet Brian to buy the garage but Brian has snatched his son Nicky and driven off with him. After Gail calls the police he later returns him.

▲ *Gail Tilsley is comforted by a policewoman after Brian kidnaps son Nicky*

► *Jenny Bradley returns home to Rita and Alan after finding love on a French holiday*

★ Mike Baldwin wants Susan to forget about a career and start a family. When Susan says she has no intention of starting one yet, Mike stays out all night.

AUGUST
★ The brewery hears from Bet, and Alec Gilroy goes to Spain where he finds her working as a waitress in Torremolinos, thinking over her problems. He proposes marriage, brings her back and becomes tenant of the Rovers.
★ Rita Fairclough thinks Alan Bradley is taking her to the register office to attend a friend's wedding. She does not know he is the groom and she is to be the bride. When she finds out, she refuses.
★ Mike sacks Susan from the shop she has opened in his factory, and she walks out on him and goes home to her father.

SEPTEMBER
★ Bet Lynch has doubts about marrying Alec but the wedding takes place with Bet in a bridal gown of ivory satin with a crinoline.
★ Tom Hopwood takes Hilda to see a bungalow at Formby and asks her to marry him, but she stalls.

OCTOBER
★ Jenny Bradley returns from France, where she went with Martin Platt to celebrate getting eight O levels. While there she falls for a young Frenchman, Patrice Podevin.

NOVEMBER
★ Susan Baldwin is pregnant and Mike is delighted, but she has an abortion, he calls her a murderer and she leaves him.
★ Derek Wilton tells Mavis Riley he has left his wife Angela and she lets him spend the night on her sofa, after which Derek scuttles back to his wife, saying he must tell her to her face.
★ Vera Duckworth suggests to Jack that they should have a lodger to occupy Terry's room at No 9. He is delighted when a pretty nurse responds to his ad, but Vera decides to install her mother, Amy Burton, in the room.
★ Hilda helps Dr and Mrs Lowther, for whom she cleans, to pack for their move to the country, after which Dr Lowther goes to fetch a takeaway meal. He returns to find his wife and Hilda unconscious, the victims of a violent robbery. Joan Lowther dies.

DECEMBER
★ Hilda leaves hospital but is nervous alone in her own house. She accepts an invitation to become Dr Lowther's housekeeper in his new home and leaves the street.
★ Jack Duckworth tells his mother-in law she ought to get a job – and then finds to his disgust that she has become the new cleaner at the Rovers.

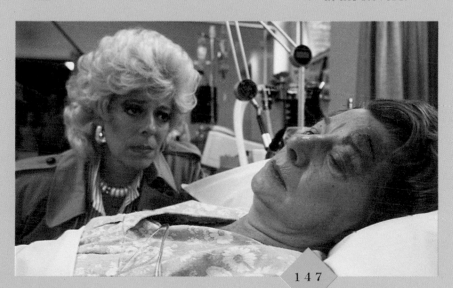

◄ *Bet Gilroy visits a battered and bruised Hilda Ogden after her terrifying ordeal at the hands of burglars at Dr and Mrs Lowther's house. Mrs Lowther dies in hospital*

1988

JANUARY

★ Mike Baldwin tells his workers that the factory has not been doing well and he is switching production from denim fashions to curtains – at lower rates of pay.

★ Alf Roberts catches Vera Duckworth's mother shoplifting from his Mini-Market. Vera's first reaction is to demand Jack give Alf a hiding, but later she tells Amy to go.

FEBRUARY

★ Mavis Riley has a date with pensioner Harry Ashton, the only applicant when the Kabin sought a new paper boy. But the teenagers object to his employment and down bags.

★ Sarah Tilsley is a year old, and Brian and Gail remarry.

★ Bet is pregnant, but suffers a miscarriage.

★ Mike Baldwin uses Gloria Todd as cover for an affair with Linda Farrell. She leaves her husband, Graham, for him, but Mike drops her, and Graham beats him up in the street.

MARCH

★ Curly Watts rents the flat above the corner shop, vacant since the Websters moved into Hilda's old home, No 13. He moves in with factory girl Shirley Armitage.

★ The street believes Audrey has left Alf, but she is in Canada caring for her son, Stephen, injured in a car crash. It is news to Gail that she has a brother. Stephen was conceived when Audrey was 16 and adopted by Malcolm Reid and his wife, who emigrated in 1962.

★ Ken Barlow is offered the chance to buy his partner Bob Statham's majority shareholding in the newspaper, but cannot manage it, and Nick Cavanagh becomes the new owner.

APRIL

★ Mike Baldwin is arrested for drink driving, is fined and disqualified, and sacks Vera for shopping him – before Ida admits it was her.

MAY

★ Alan Bradley opens his own burglar alarm firm in offices acquired with a £6,000 loan from Rita.

★ Percy Sugden is told that now he is 65 he has to retire as caretaker of the community centre. Percy becomes a lollipop man in Bessie Street.

JUNE
★ Cab driver Don Brennan and Ivy Tilsley marry, with Jack Duckworth as Don's best man.
★ New *Recorder* owner Nick Cavanagh flees the country, leaving his daughter Fiona and junior partner Ken Barlow to face creditors, chief of whom is Statham. Ken now buys him out for £20,000.

JULY
★ Ronnie Stubbs comes home from sea seeking his wife Sandra, a new cleaner at the Rovers, who left him because he beat her. She is persuaded to meet him – and he puts her in hospital.

AUGUST
★ Bet takes in a stray Alsatian as a guard dog, naming it Rover. It does not like Alec and he pays a boy to claim the animal.
★ Terry Duckworth returns, looking affluent, wearing an expensive watch and gold jewellery.

SEPTEMBER
★ Curly Watts elects to study Baldwin's factory as a research project for his business studies college course. Curly alleges it is a sweat shop and Ken Barlow puts the story on the front page.

★ Derek Wilton proposes to Mavis through the Kabin letterbox and she accepts.

OCTOBER
★ Alec Gilroy reports that a mugger robbed him of £6,000, the pub's weekend takings, but few people believe his story.
★ Vera buys a bed, a microwave and a washing machine with the compensation Jack gets from suing her after an injury he suffered when she crashed her car.

NOVEMBER
★ Alan Bradley leaves Rita after she discovers he is having an affair with Carole Burns, but Rita begs him to return to her.
★ Mavis and Derek marry, and make their home in her flat over the Kabin.

DECEMBER
★ Deirdre Barlow is approached, as a councillor, by unemployed Brian Roscoe, facing Christmas in a high-rise slum flat. She decides to take presents for his two children but Roscoe, who is mentally ill, holds her prisoner until she escapes in the early hours of Christmas morning.
★ Don Brennan wins £60 from Mike Baldwin in a poker game, but in a return game Don bets and loses his cab, and Ivy has to use £1,000 of her savings to get it back.

◄ *Brian and Gail Tilsley remarry as daughter Sarah celebrates her first birthday. They hope to rekindle the flames of their early years together, and young Nicky is grateful to have a real father again*

◄ *Rovers cleaner Sandra Stubbs gives some advice to barmaid Gloria Todd, who is being two-timed by Mike Baldwin. Sandra has her own man problems, courtesy of her violent husband*

1989

JANUARY

★ Planning to open a shop to sell his burglar alarm equipment, Alan Bradley plots to raise the money by taking out a second mortgage on No 7 – Rita Fairclough's home – calling himself Mr Fairclough when he phones the building society.

★ Alec Gilroy has problems with the tax men, but he has a show business deal acting as tour manager for a group of entertainers including exotic dancer Tanya, on a nine-week Middle East tour.

FEBRUARY

★ Brian Tilsley's nights on the town are being talked about, and Gail tells him she wants another divorce. But then Brian is killed, stabbed by one of a bunch of yobs who trap him with a blonde in a dark alley outside a club.

★ Paper boy Jason Stubbs entertains friends while his mother is working at the Rovers, their games become rowdy, and Jason is injured.

MARCH

★ When Alan Bradley sacks Dawn Prescott, she tells Rita that Alan tried to rape her. When Rita confronts him about this and the fraudulent use of her deeds to raise a loan, he tries to kill her.

★ Tom Casey makes Gail an offer of £18,500 for Brian's garage. Kevin is unable to match it, and Casey becomes his boss.

APRIL

★ Curly and Shirley part after a year together which Curly has spent studying and Shirley has spent slaving at the factory to earn enough for both of them.

★ Derek's company doctor diagnoses him as showing signs of stress and when he threatens resignation it is accepted and he breaks down.

MAY

★ Alec Gilroy comes home unexpectedly from the desert and catches Bet out with Paul Rigby. He demands a divorce, sacks Bet and brings in Tanya, the exotic dancer, otherwise Megan Morgan.

★ Desperate for employment, Derek Wilton takes a job as a salesman selling jokes and novelties.

★ Don Brennan accepts a greyhound named Harry's Luck in payment for a 30-mile taxi ride. Lucky makes its debut at the track but does not run well and is found to be pregnant.

JUNE

★ Ken Barlow acquires some scoops on confidential council business. Deirdre is suspected of being his informant and is asked to leave a committee meeting – but Ken still manages to print details of it.

★ Alec and Bet are reconciled as Megan goes.

★ Gail Tilsley pays £9,000 to become an equal partner in Jim's Café with Alma Sedgewick, who is spending most of her time pursuing Mike Baldwin.

JULY

★ Kevin Webster and Tom Casey's son, Mark, plan to take up banger racing but clash over who will drive the car and decide on a time trial. Kevin is faster than Mark, but Sally is faster still.

★ Alma Sedgewick gets Mike Baldwin into bed after bearing him at golf, but Mike dumps her for Dawn Prescott, and Alma starts an affair with married Terry Conway.

★ Jack Duckworth asks barmaid Tina Fowler for a date, and for a laugh she agrees, after which Vera insults her in the Rovers.

★ Don Brennan sells greyhound Lucky and her pups for £800.

AUGUST

★ Mike Baldwin sells his factory to Maurice Jones and staff suddenly find the gates locked. Mike moves into a new dockland flat.

SEPTEMBER

★ Wendy Crozier is sacked from the Town Hall for leaking information to Ken, and he offers her a job on the *Recorder*. They soon begin an affair.

★ The factory is demolished and Emily organises all-girl pickets of the site in a fight for redundancy money.

◄ *Alan Bradley is found guilty of fraud and assault but goes free, having served seven months*

▼ *Rita Fairclough comforts Alan's daughter, but Jenny blames Rita for her father's plight*

OCTOBER

★ Widowed Gail Tilsley has been comforted by young Martin Platt and spends a night with him.

★ At his trial Alan Bradley pleads guilty to assaulting Rita, and because he has already spent six months in custody, walks free. He returns to Weatherfield, finds lodgings and a job as a builder's labourer.

★ Audrey Roberts tries to persuade Alf to leave Coronation Street for an upmarket dockland flat, and smartens No 11 for a quick sale at £25,000.

NOVEMBER

★ The Kabin is burgled and Rita Fairclough blames Alan Bradley, convinced he is trying to intimidate her. Rita disappears and Mavis calls the police, who question Bradley and search his flat, as a result of which he loses his job.

★ In the Rovers Eddie Ramsden, one of Maurice Jones's building site workers, tries to chat up Tina Fowler and provokes a punch-up in which Kevin and Curly are hurt.

★ Dawn Prescott is visited by her brother Robert, who tells Mike it is possible to make a million in Spain. Mike flies there to beat Prescott in a deal, buying land for £150,000.

DECEMBER

★ Mike Baldwin finds he has bought the land from Robert and it is worthless. He blames Dawn and throws her out.

★ Vera Duckworth gets her redundancy cheque – nearly £2,000 – but she loses her supermarket job after new executive Curly Watts writes assessments of the staff's work. Curly then loses his lodgings with the Duckworths.

★ Bet finds Rita Fairclough singing in a piano bar in Blackpool and suffering from loss of memory. Alan Bradley follows and sees Rita in the street. She runs, he chases her and is knocked down and killed by a tram.

★ Alf and Audrey leave Coronation Street and Jim and Liz McDonald and their 15 year old twins Andy and Steve move in. But Alf and Audrey's flat purchase falls through and they have to return and live above the shop.

1990

JANUARY

★ Deirdre discovers Ken's affair with Wendy Crozier, sees a solicitor and throws him out. Wendy takes him in.

★ Alec persuades Bet to accompany him to Cheshire to attend the birthday party of his long-lost daughter Sandra.

★ Mike Baldwin, cleaned out by his Spanish land deal, is trying to build a new business. He has an order but no factory and no work-force. Alma Sedgewick becomes his live-in lover.

FEBRUARY

★ No 6, the first home in the Street's new housing development, is bought by bookie Desmond Barnes and his wife Stephanie, to move into immediately after their Valentine Day wedding.

★ Ex-soldier Jim McDonald, recently moved into No 11, is having second thoughts about civilian life and considers re-enlisting in a recruiting job against the wishes of wife Liz.

★ Mavis Wilton's one-time suitor Victor

Pendlebury sends Derek to Bedford on an overnight business trip. Derek returns to find Victor trying to seduce her.

MARCH

★ Marie Lancaster, the mother of Eddie Ramsden's son, confronts Eddie's girlfriend Tina Fowler in a bid to get Jamie back.

★ Alf and Audrey Roberts leave the Street.

★ Steph Barnes sets her cap at Kevin and shaves off his moustache at a party, after which the Websters quarrel.

★ Ken Barlow sells the *Recorder* to pay off his mortgage so that Deirdre can have their home. He takes a job on the free-sheet *Gazette* but clashes with the editor and becomes unemployed.

★ Mavis and Derek move out of the Kabin to their new home across the street, but she mourns the death of her budgie, Harriet.

◀ *Alma Sedgewick moves in with Mike Baldwin after Dawn Prescott walks out on him*

▲ *Don Brennan is under suspicion of a hit-and-run incident but he's eventually cleared*

▼ *Reeling from husband Ken's affair with Wendy Crozier, Deirdre Barlow comes face to face with the former council secretary who leaked secrets to the* Recorder

WHO'S WHO IN THE STREET TODAY

MIKE BALDWIN (Johnny Briggs)
A Bermondsey boy who started in the rag trade in London and moved to Weatherfield in 1976, making denim clothes and later curtains, until he sold the factory in 1989. He then lost all his money in a Spanish land deal. But he is a man who will always bounce back. A cockney casanova, he married Susan Barlow, young enough to be his daughter, in 1986, but they parted when she refused to have children. Has since taken up with Alma Sedgewick.

KEN BARLOW (William Roache)
Showed great promise at school and university, where he took a degree in history. He was a rebel, jailed for taking part in an anti-Vietnam war demo in 1967. He held a variety of jobs, from teacher to community development officer, before becoming editor and eventually owner of the *Weatherfield Recorder*, but then sold out. Married three times: in 1962 to Valerie Tatlock, who gave birth to twins but died of electrocution; in 1973 to Janet Reid, with whom he split up and she later died of a drug overdose; and in 1981 to Deirdre Langton, who threw him out in 1989 because of his affair with Wendy Crozier.

▲ *Tracy Barlow has seen her mother's marriages to Ray Langton and Ken Barlow both break up*

DEIRDRE BARLOW (Anne Kirkbride)
As 18-year-old dollybird Deirdre Hunt, she was a typist for Len Fairclough and Ray Langton. She married Langton in 1975 and their daughter Tracy was born in 1977. After divorce, she married Ken Barlow and became stepmother to his two children, but they split up over his affair with Wendy Crozier. She is a Weatherfield councillor and lives at No 1.

DES and **STEPH BARNES** (Philip Middlemiss and Amelia Bullmore)
The first couple to move into the new No 6 Coronation Street in 1990, which they did immediately after their wedding, and before their honeymoon. He is a bookmaker, she sells cosmetics.

▲ *Des and Steph Barnes are the pranksters who bring unpredictable fun to the* Street

EMILY BISHOP (Eileen Derbyshire)
Formerly Emily Nugent, straitlaced daughter of an ex-Indian army officer, she has spent her working life in the rag trade. As Baldwin's book-keeper at the factory, she led the fight for redundancy money. She married photographer Ernest Bishop in 1972, but he was killed in a wages snatch in 1978. A marriage to Arnold Swain in 1980 turned out to be bigamous. Lives at No 3.

JENNY BRADLEY (Sally Ann Matthews)
She was a paper girl at the Kabin when she learned that her mother had been killed in a road accident. This brought her father, Alan, back into her life after she had not seen him for eight years, and she remained loyally defensive of him until some time after his death. After gaining A-levels, she went to Manchester Polytechnic to read environmental studies. Lives at No 7.

DON and **IVY BRENNAN** (Geoff Hinsliff and Lynne Perrie)
A card-playing cabbie with a son and two daughters by his former wife Pat, he married Ivy Tilsley in 1988, and they live at No 5. The abrasive widow of Bert Tilsley, and mother of Brian, she was a shop steward at Mike Baldwin's factory until its sale.

MARK CASEY (Stuart Wolfenden)
Teenage son of Tom Casey, who bought Brian Tilsley's garage, installing Mark as Kevin Webster's assistant. Kevin sacked him for not pulling his weight, but he was reinstated and persuaded Kevin to join him in banger racing.

▶ *Garage mechanic Mark Casey thinks himself the world's authority on women, but his smooth-talking manner does not always work*

JACK and VERA DUCKWORTH (William Tarmey and Elizabeth Dawn)

Cellarman at the Rovers, previously a van and cab driver, medallion man Jack is well-meaning but lazy and gullible. He is married to gum-chewing, foghorn-voiced Vera, who has worked in a supermarket since losing her job as a machinist in Mike Baldwin's factory. Parents of the ne'er-do-well Terry, born 1964, they live at No 9, bickering constantly.

RITA FAIRCLOUGH (Barbara Knox)

Former exotic dancer and club singer, she married Len Fairclough in 1977 but was widowed in 1983 and inherited the Kabin newsagent's, with a flat above it. Has since bought a new shop in Coronation Street. Her decision to foster Jenny Bradley led to an association with Alan Bradley, who nearly killed her before his own death.

REG HOLDSWORTH (Ken Morley)

The son of a grocer, Reg Holdsworth is manager of Bettabuys supermarket, in Albert Road, Weatherfield. His wife threw him out of the house when she found out about his affair with store detective Renee Dodds. He was discovered sleeping in the supermarket storeroom by his assistant manager, Curly Watts, and found refuge in the flat over Alf Roberts's Mini-Market in Coronation Street.

ALEC and BET GILROY (Roy Barraclough and Julie Goodyear)

Landlord and landlady of the Rovers Return. He was an on-the-make club owner and theatrical agent who lent Bet the money to buy the tenancy of the Rovers. When she disappeared, he tracked her down in Spain, where he found her waitressing. A proposal of marriage meant the brewery would happily give him the tenancy and she could remain landlady. Bet originally worked at the raincoat factory, then in a launderette, before becoming a barmaid at the Rovers. She had an illegitimate son, Martin, killed in a road crash while serving in the Army in Northern Ireland.

JIM and LIZ McDONALD (Charles Lawson and Beverley Callard)

Ex-soldier Jim and wife Liz moved into No 11 at the end of 1989 with their 14-year-old twin sons Andy and Steve, soon in trouble for breaking windows at the Mini Market.

PHYLLIS PEARCE (Jill Summers)

Bossy, blue-rinsed pensioner, washer-up at the café, sacked by Alma Sedgewick in 1989. Her husband, Harold, died in 1976 and her daughter, Mary, the following year, but she has a grandson, Craig, born 1967. Has pursued Percy Sugden fruitlessly.

MARTIN PLATT (Sean Wilson)

Studied confectionery at Salford Tech, but after leaving in 1984 spent a year on the dole before he got a job at Jim's Café in 1985, when he was 16. Later worked for Alan Bradley's security firm, taking a night job at a petrol station after Bradley's arrest. Has since become a hospital porter. Jenny Bradley made a play for him, but he said she was too young for him and started an affair with widow Gail Tilsley.

ALF and AUDREY ROBERTS (Bryan Mosley and Sue Nicholls)

Alf, a retired Post Office supervisor, runs the Mini Market and is a former Councillor and pillar of the community. He has been married three times. His first wife, Phyllis Plant, died in 1972, after which he married Renee Bradshaw, owner of the corner shop in 1978 and inherited the business when she died in a car crash two years later. He was snapped up by Audrey Potter, who had two illegitimate children, Stephen and Gail, when she was young. Alf had a heart attack in 1987.

▲ *Moving to the street meant Jim McDonald could come home to wife Liz and civilian life*

ALMA SEDGEWICK (Amanda Barrie)
Divorced from husband Jim, she became owner of Jim's Café, which she now runs in partnership with Gail Tilsley. An affair with Mike Baldwin began after she beat him at golf.

PERCY SUGDEN (Bill Waddington)
A formerly Army cook, he was caretaker of the community centre until he was retired at 65, when he became a lollipop man. A busybody with a mania for organising anything from Neighbourhood Watch schemes to formation dance classes, he lodges with Emily Bishop at No 3.

GAIL TILSLEY (Helen Worth)
The illegitimate daughter of Audrey Roberts, father unknown, she worked at the warehouse as clerk typist, and later at Sylvia's Separates. Married Brian Tilsley and had children Nicky and Sarah Louise. After his death, found consolation with 'toyboy' Martin Platt. A partner in the café.

BETTY TURPIN (Betty Driver)
Gossipy former mill girl and school meals assistant, widow of police Sgt Cyril Turpin, who died in 1974. Barmaid at the Rovers (on and off) since 1969. Has illegitimate son, Gordon, adopted by her sister Maggie Clegg, who formerly kept the corner shop but has since married Ron Cooke and gone to live in Zaire.

CURLY WATTS (Kevin Kennedy)
His real name is Norman, but he is known as Curly because of his straight hair. The bespectacled egg-head of the Street (eight O-levels and two A-levels), he turned down university to earn cash and was in business with Terry Duckworth, selling door-to-door, but after a business course became a supermarket executive. Formerly lived with Shirley Armitage. Hobby: astronomy. Lodges with the Duckworths.

KEVIN and SALLY WEBSTER (Michael Le Vell and Sally Whittaker)
Kevin became a mechanic at Brian Tilsley's garage in 1983 and married Sally Seddon in 1986. Sally, once a cheeky flirt, now a charmer and working in the corner shop, is ambitious for the cheerful but cautious Kevin. Both look forward to becoming parents. They live at No 13.

DEREK and MAVIS WILTON (Peter Baldwin and Thelma Barlow)
Derek was a stationery sales rep and met Mavis Riley when he called at the Kabin for orders in 1976. They planned to marry in 1984, but both got cold feet and he later married someone else. That ended in divorce and he married Mavis in 1988. He became a salesman of toys and novelties, before joining Victor Pendlebury's paper products company. Once dubbed the eternal virgin, Mavis has written a novel, *Song of a Scarlet Summer*, and won a competition for a radio short story in collaboration with Victor Pendlebury. They live at No 4.

◄ *Gail Tilsley and children Nicky and Sarah remain together despite a turbulent past*

ROLL CALL
THE CAST

Coronation Street's main characters, past and present

● indicates a member of the original cast in 1960
+ indicates a member of the cast in 1990

● Christine Appleby	CHRISTINE HARGREAVES
Colin Appleby	LAURENCE JAMES
Shirley Armitage	LISA LEWIS
+Mike Baldwin	JOHNNY BRIGGS
Susan Baldwin	WENDY JANE WALKER
● David Barlow	ALAN ROTHWELL
+Deirdre Barlow	ANNE KIRKBRIDE
● Frank Barlow	FRANK PEMBERTON
● Ida Barlow	NOEL DYSON
Irma Barlow	SANDRA GOUGH
● +Ken Barlow	WILLIAM ROACHE
Janet Barlow	JUDITH BARKER
Peter Barlow	JOHN HEANUS/MARK DUNCAN/CHRIS DORMES/ LINUS ROACHE/JOSEPH McKENNA/DAVID LONSDALE
Susan Barlow	*see Susan Baldwin*, plus KATIE HEANUE, SUSAN PATTERSON
+Tracy Barlow	CHRISTABEL FINCH/HOLLY CHAMARETTE/DAWN ACTON
Valerie Barlow	ANNE REID
+Des Barnes	PHILIP MIDDLEMISS
+Steph Barnes	AMELIA BULLMORE
Sir Julius Berlin	LEONARD SACHS
Suzie Birchall	CHERYL MURRAY
+Emily Bishop	EILEEN DERBYSHIRE
Ernie Bishop	STEPHEN HANCOCK
Jerry Booth	GRAHAM HABERFIELD
Myra Booth	SUSAN JAMESON
Alan Bradley	MARK EDEN
Frank Bradley	TOMMY BOYLE
Jenny Bradley	SALLY ANN MATTHEWS
Terry Bradshaw	BOB MASON
+Don Brennan	GEOFF HINSLIFF
+Ivy Brennan	LYNNE PERRIE
Vicki Bright	CLAIRE SUTCLIFFE
Amy Burton	FANNY CARBY
Bernard Butler	GORDEN KAYE
Sandra Butler	PATRICIA FULLER
● Minnie Caldwell	MARGOT BRYANT
+Mark Casey	STUART WOLFENDEN
Tom Casey	EDWARD CLAYTON
● Ivan Cheveski	ERNST WALDER
● Linda Cheveski	ANNE CUNNINGHAM
Martin Cheveski	JONATHON CAPLAN
Paul Cheveski	MARCUS SAVILLE
Jasmine Choong	LUCILLE SOONG
Andrea Clayton	CAROLINE O'NEILL
Connie Clayton	SUSAN BROWN
Harry Clayton	JOHNNY LEEZE
Sue Clayton	JANE HAZLEGROVE
Gordon Clegg	BILL KENWRIGHT
Les Clegg	JOHN SHARP
Maggie Clegg	*see Maggie Cooke*
Ida Clough	HELENE PALMER
Maggie Cooke	IRENE SUTCLIFFE
Ron Cooke	ERIC LANDER
Archie Crabtree	JOHN STRATTON

Norman Crabtree	STAN STENNETT
Neil Crossley	GEOFFREY MATTHEWS
Sheila Crossley	EILEEN MYERS
+Wendy Crozier	ROBERTA KERR
● Susan Cunningham	PATRICIA SHAKESBY
Tommy Deakin	PADDY JOYCE
Dirty Dick	TALFRYN THOMAS
Joe Donnelli	SHANE RIMMER
+Jack Duckworth	WILLIAM TARMEY
Terry Duckworth	NIGEL PIVARO
+Vera Duckworth	ELIZABETH DAWN
Maggie Dunlop	*see Maggie Redman*
Len Fairclough	PETER ADAMSON
+Rita Fairclough	BARBARA KNOX
Stanley Fairclough	PETER NOONE/JONATHAN COY
Steve Fisher	LAWRENCE MULLEN
Audrey Fleming	GILLIAN McCANN
Dickie Fleming	NIGEL HUMPHRIES
Gregg Flint	BILL NAGY
Jacko Ford	ROBERT KEEGAN
Norma Ford	DIANA DAVIES
+Tina Fowler	MICHELLE HOLMES
Laurie Fraser	STANLEY MEADOWS
Dulcie Froggatt	MARJI CAMPI
Handel Gartside	HARRY MARKHAM
Sharon Gaskell	TRACIE BENNETT
Edna Gee	MAVIS ROGERSON
Eunice Gee	MEG JOHNSON
Fred Gee	FRED FEAST
+Alec Gilroy	ROY BARRACLOUGH
+Bet Gilroy	JULIE GOODYEAR
Dot Greenhalgh	JOAN FRANCIS
Bill Gregory	JACK WATSON
Marjorie Griffin	MARJIE LAWRENCE
Christine Hardman	*see Christine Appleby*
May Hardman	JOAN HEATH
Frank Harvey	NICK STRINGER
Nellie Harvey	MOLLIE SUGDEN
Esther Hayes	DAPHNE OXENFORD
Tom Hayes	DUDLEY FOSTER
Concepta Hewitt	*see Concepta Regan*
● Harry Hewitt	IVAN BEAVIS
Lucille Hewitt	JENNIFER MOSS
Reg Holdsworth	KEN MORLEY
Granny Hopkins	JESSIE EVANS
Idris Hopkins	RICHARD DAVIES
Tricia Hopkins	KATHY JONES
Vera Hopkins	KATHY STAFF
Tom Hopwood	LEN MARTEN
Alan Howard	ALAN BROWNING
Elsie Howard	*see Elsie Tanner*
Blanche Hunt	MAGGIE JONES
Deirdre Hunt	*see Deirdre Barlow*
Dan Johnson	RICHARD SHAW
+Maurice Jones	ALAN MOORE

+Felicity Khan RITA WOLF

Deirdre Langton *see Deirdre Barlow*
Janice Langton PAULA WILCOX
Ray Langton NEVILLE BUSWELL
Tracy Langton *see Tracy Barlow*
● Elsie Lappin MAUDIE EDWARDS
Ian Latimer MICHAEL LONEY
Nancy Leathers NORAH HAMMOND
Gordon Lewis DAVID DAKER
● Florrie Lindley BETTY ALBERGE
Vera Lomax RUTH HOLDEN
● Martha Longhurst LYNNE CAROL
Doreen Lostock ANGELA CROW
Bet Lynch *see Bet Gilroy*

+Andy McDonald NICHOLAS COCHRANE
+Jim McDonald CHARLES LAWSON
+Liz McDonald BEVERLEY CALLARD
Steve McDonald SIMON GREGORY
Frank Mills NIGEL GREGORY
Charlie Moffitt GORDON ROLLINGS
Megan Morgan SUE RODERICK
Jim Mount BARRY KEAGAN
Tickler Murphy PATRICK McALLINNEY

Wendy Nightingale SUSAN TEBBS
Emily Nugent *see Emily Bishop*

Hilda Ogden JEAN ALEXANDER
Irma Ogden *see Irma Barlow*
Polly Ogden MARY TAMM
Stan Ogden BERNARD YOUENS
Trevor Ogden JONATHAN COLLINS/DON HAWKINS

+Phyllis Pearce JILL SUMMERS
Beattie Pearson GABRIELLE DAYE
Victor Pendlebury CHRISTOPHER COLL
Elaine Perkins JOANNA LUMLEY
Lionel Petty EDWARD EVANS
Sandra Petty HEATHER MOORE
Alice Pickens DORIS HARE
William Piggott GEORGE A. COOPER
+Martin Platt SEAN WILSON
Walter Potts CHRIS SANDFORD
Dawn Prescott LOUISE HARRISON
Elaine Prior *see Elaine Webster*

Maggie Redman JILL KERMAN
Concepta Regan DOREEN KEOGH
Janet Reid *see Janet Barlow*
Stella Rigby VIVIENNE ROSS
Brenda Riley EILEEN KENNALLY
Concepta Riley *see Concepta Regan*
Mavis Riley *see Mavis Wilton*
+Alf Roberts BRYAN MOSLEY
+Audrey Roberts SUE NICHOLLS
Renee Roberts MADGE HINDLE
Gertie Robson CONNIE MERRIGOLD

Elsie Seddon BRENDA ELDER
Gina Seddon JULIE FOY
Sally Seddon *see Sally Whittaker*
+Alma Sedgewick AMANDA BARRIE
Jim Sedgewick MICHAEL O'HAGAN
● Ena Sharples VIOLET CARSON
Dave Smith REGINALD MARSH
John Spencer JONATHAN BARKER
Effie Spicer ANNE DYSON
Jean Stark RENNY LISTER
Jed Stone KENNETH COPE
Sandra Stubbs SALLY WATTS
+Percy Sugden BILL WADDINGTON
Jenny Sutton *see Jenny Tanner*
Arnold Swain GEORGE WARING
Leonard Swindley ARTHUR LOWE

Arnold Tanner FRANK CRAWSHAW
● Dennis Tanner PHILIP LOWRIE
● Elsie Tanner PATRICIA PHOENIX
Jenny Tanner MITZI ROGERS
Steve Tanner PAUL MAXWELL
Wally Tanner GEORGE BETTON
● Albert Tatlock JACK HOWARTH
Valerie Tatlock *see Valerie Barlow*
+Kimberley Taylor SUZANNE HALL
Bert Tilsley PETER DUDLEY
Brian Tilsley CHRISTOPHER QUINTEN
+Gail Tilsley HELEN WORTH
Ivy Tilsley *see Ivy Brennan*
+Nicky Tilsley WARREN JACKSON
+Sarah Louise Tilsley LYNSAY KING
Sam Tindall TOM MENNARD
Gloria Todd SUE JENKINS
+Betty Turpin BETTY DRIVER
Cyril Turpin WILLIAM MOORE

Henry Wakefield FINETIME FONTAYNE
● Annie Walker DORIS SPEED
Billy Walker KENNETH FARRINGTON
● Jack Walker ARTHUR LESLIE
Joan Walker *see Joan Davies*
George Wardle RON DAVIS
+Curly Watts KEVIN KENNEDY
Bill Webster PETER ARMITAGE
Debbie Webster SUE DEVANEY
Elaine Webster JUDY GRIDLEY
+Kevin Webster MICHAEL LE VELL
+Sally Webster SALLY WHITTAKER
Bob Whiteley FREDDIE FLETCHER
Chalkie Whiteley TEDDY TURNER
Craig Whiteley MARK PRICE
Marion Willis *see Marion Yeats*
+Derek Wilton PETER BALDWIN
+Mavis Wilton THELMA BARLOW

Eddie Yeats GEOFFREY HUGHES
Marion Yeats VERONICA DORAN

Miklos Zadic PAUL STASSINO

▲ *A visit by Prime Minister Margaret Thatcher*
draws the locals to the Rovers